MRS
BEETON
CLASSIC
MEAT
DISHES

Mrs Beeton How to Cook

Mrs Beeton Soups & Sides

Mrs Beeton Fish & Seafood

Mrs Beeton Chicken, Other Birds & Game

Mrs Beeton Classic Meat Dishes

Mrs Beeton Cakes & Bakes

Mrs Beeton Puddings

MRS BEETON CLASSIC MEAT DISHES

ISABELLA BEETON & GERARD BAKER

FOREWORD BY FERGUS HENDERSON

For my grandmothers Nora Baker and Elsie Hinch,
who spanned the gap between Isabella and me.

Gerard Baker

This edition published in Great Britain in 2012 by Weidenfeld & Nicolson
Originally published in 2011 by Weidenfeld & Nicolson as part of *Mrs Beeton How to Cook*

1 3 5 7 9 10 8 6 4 2

Text copyright © Weidenfeld & Nicolson 2012
Design and layout copyright © Weidenfeld & Nicolson 2012

Design & Art Direction by Julyan Bayes
Photography by Andrew Hayes-Watkins
Illustration by Bold & Noble. Additional illustration by Carol Kearns
Food Styling by Sammy-Jo Squire
Prop Styling by Giuliana Casarotti
Edited by Zelda Turner

A CIP catalogue record for this book is available from the British Library.
ISBN 978 0 297 86683 1

The Orion Publishing Group's policy is to use papers that are natural, renewable and recyclable products and made from wood grown in sustainable forests. The logging and manufacturing processes are expected to conform to the environmental regulations of the country of origin.

Printed and bound in Spain

Weidenfeld & Nicolson
The Orion Publishing Group Ltd
Orion House
5 Upper St Martin's Lane
London WC2H 9EA

An Hachette UK Company

www.orionbooks.co.uk

CONTENTS

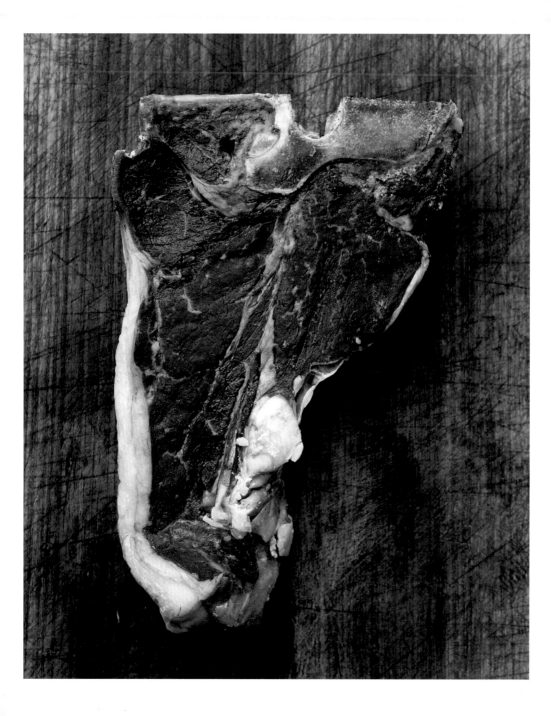

FOREWORD

If Mrs Beeton found herself whisked away in a time machine to today's London, I think she would be surprised by the way we buy our meat. She obviously wouldn't have an Oyster card; so much walking would be required to find the nearest butcher's shop.

Of course, the fact that every nation's food is represented would soften the blow. But when she searched for a butcher (or a wet fish shop) she would find them few and far between. It's the knowledge of the carcass that is important: how long it's been hung, understanding the offal. All this has gone with the demise of the butcher.

Imagine Mrs Beeton dazzled by the bright lights of the supermarkets and the many delights on sale within. She finds the meat finally, with some difficulty, as it's all pink, anonymous and in plastic. No jellied pig's cheeks here.

Disappointed, she heads out and eats a Vietnamese supper on the Kingsland Road. Things are looking up.

She checks herself into an inn on the Boundary and spends most of the night grappling with the television remote. On discovering the mini bar, she does her best to empty it. In the morning, despite her frail state, the innkeeper rather roughly sends her out onto the street, saying, 'Your ha'penny is no good to us here!' Mrs Beeton thought it was a fairly generous offer, having done battle with some very strange furniture in her room.

She walks to Spitalfields market, which she has always relied on to find a good soused pig's head. Coming upon a simple but fine hostelry on Commercial Street, she lunches on a brace of herring on oatmeal, a rabbit and trotter pie, and pressed pig's cheeks. And a few bumpers of Burgundy.

She stands and gives a toast to the Queen 'Victoria'. The rest of the restaurant replies with muffled embarrassment, 'Elizabeth'.

It suddenly comes to me, 'Blimey that's Mrs Beeton'. But before I have time to walk over to her and ask, 'Do things seem better or worse?', the dammed time machine has whisked her back to the 19th century.

Ach well, we still have her writings, her recipes and remedies.

Fergus Henderson

THE INIMITABLE MRS BEETON

When Isabella Beeton first published *Beeton's Book of Household Management* in 1861, Britain was changing from a rural society, in which large numbers of people were involved in farming and many grew their own fruit and vegetables at home, to an industrialised one, where the development of modern transport networks, refrigeration and kitchen appliances brought a world of food to our fingertips.

Today, most of us have an image of Mrs Beeton as a matronly figure – brisk, efficient and experienced in the kitchen. In fact, Isabella Beeton was young and recently married, juggling working outside the home with running her household and coping with the demands of a husband and young family. Having worked on it throughout her early twenties, she saw her book published at the age of 25 and died just three years later.

Although she wrote of housekeepers, butlers and valets, her semi-detached in Hatch End was a world away from the big country houses of the preceding century, and although it is likely that she had some help in the kitchen, she almost certainly managed her home and most of the cooking herself. Her book was inspired by an awareness of the challenges faced by women like herself – and with that in mind, she used her position as editor of *The Englishwoman's Domestic Magazine* to pull together the best recipes and advice from a wide range of sources.

She was among the first revolutionary food writers to style recipes in the format that we are familiar with today, setting out clear lists of ingredients and details of time taken, average cost and portions produced (this last being entirely her invention). She also offered notes on how to source the best food for her recipes – placing particular emphasis on such old-fashioned (or, in our eyes, surprisingly modern) ideas as the use of seasonal, local produce and the importance of animal welfare.

It is easy to see why Mrs Beeton's core themes – buy well, cook well and eat well – are as relevant today as they were 150 years ago. Her original book was written with an awareness of household economy that we can take lessons from too. Because we have access to so much so easily, we often forget to consider how to get the most out of each ingredient – yet maximising flavour and nutrient value and minimising waste is as relevant in the twenty-first century as it was in 1861.

The right ingredients

Mrs Beeton's original recipes have needed careful adaptation. In some cases, the modern recipes are amalgamations of more than one Beeton recipe or suggestion, which I hope give a more coherent whole. Many of the ingredients that may seem at first glance universal are so different today from those varieties Isabella would have been familiar with that using them in the original way can give quite different results to those intended. For those reasons, quantities needed to be not only converted but checked and altered. And all those cases where Mrs Beeton advised adding salt or sugar or honey or spices 'to taste' have been pinned down in real quantities, always keeping in mind both flavour and authenticity.

In the case of many of the meat and fish dishes in particular, the modern recipes are amalgamations of more than one Beeton recipe or suggestion. Where a Victorian cook would have happily chosen a plain meat from one chapter and a sauce from another, we tend to prefer the convenience of having everything in one place.

Cooking methods, too, were in some cases not replicable and in others simply no longer the best way of achieving the desired results. A significant factor in this is that the domestic oven was in its infancy in 1861, and Mrs Beeton was not able to make full use of it in her book. Most kitchens would instead have been equipped with old-fashioned ranges, and there is much mention of setting things before the fire, turning and basting. Roasting meat, which we now consider a simple process, required constant attention 150 years ago. Oven temperatures, therefore, have all had to be deduced from a mixture of reading between the lines, comparing modern recipes, and testing, testing, testing.

The end result, however, has been to produce dishes that Mrs Beeton would, hopefully, have been happy to call her own.

The legacy

After Isabella Beeton died early in 1865, her book took on a life of its own. It was endlessly enlarged, modern recipes were added and eventually, in the many, many editions of the book that have been published in the past 150 years, the spirit of the original was lost.

The picture of British food that Isabella painted in the first edition was about to change wholesale, and her book was destined to change with it. The aim of this collection is to reverse those changes: to return to real, wholesome, traditional British food, which Mrs Beeton might be proud to recognise as her own – and to put to rest the matronly image.

INTRODUCTION

R ed meat has always been popular in the UK, and there is a long history of association between Englishmen and beef. Historically, however, the most economical animal to rear for meat, and therefore the most commonly consumed, was the pig, which provides a large quantity of versatile fat in addition to a variety of cuts of meat. It also produces large litters. Cows were valued for their milk and so would have been killed only when their milking days had passed, or when an event warranted it. Sheep, too, were often not butchered until they had aged, which partly explains why our collective memory of mutton is of a scraggy beast, because these were the only animals that would have been eaten by most people. Properly raised mutton gives a rich, aromatic meat without too much fat; lamb, by comparison, is tender and delicate.

The development of animal breeds

Different breeds are valued for their individual characteristics. For example, some breeds of cattle are prized for the flavour or tenderness of their meat, others for their high milk production. Still others, mountain cattle for example, are esteemed for their ability to produce meat on poor land where most other breeds would not thrive.

Unfortunately, the majority of the beef and pork we eat today comes from breeds that are chosen for their ability to mature quickly, producing a large quantity of meat in a relatively short time. Pigs and sheep usually reach the market within their first year; beef animals can be up to 30 months old before they are killed, but even that is very young compared to the age at which animals would have been killed at the time Mrs Beeton was writing her book. However, an increasing number of farms are now reviving traditional breeds known for their characterful meat, and these are well worth tracking down at farm shops or farmers' markets (see producers & suppliers page 91).

Sheep are not usually farmed as intensively as cows and pigs, so breed distribution remains much more varied, even in the meat that reaches supermarket shelves.

The majority of the meat we buy comes from conventional (including free-range) and factory production, with organically reared animals making up a small, but increasing, proportion of total sales. Most livestock are fed on grass or cereal and soya-based foods milled to precise nutritional specifications. Free-range animals, particularly those reared on old pasture, benefit from a more varied diet, and this is reflected in the vastly superior flavour of the meat.

Meat raised under strict free-range specifications will be labelled as such. Some meat also carries the RSPCA Freedom Food mark, indicating that the animals have been well cared for to certain recognised standards.

The ageing process

Beef, lamb and mutton benefit from hanging, a process of slow drying that concentrates and enriches the flavour of the flesh. Pork is generally not hung because the animal's skin deteriorates in condition during the process. Lamb should be hung for at least ten days; beef for a minimum of three weeks and up to five weeks, at a low temperature just above freezing.

Curing

Salting or pickling, also called curing, is a centuries-old method of preserving meat to extend the length of time it can be stored. Although we now have the option of freezing meat to preserve it, curing adds flavour, texture and character, and you can do it at home.

There are so many traditional methods of brining in the British Isles that you can experiment forever. A good place to start, however, is with the simple recipe for curing bacon on page 63, which is based on Mrs Beeton's Westmorland cure for ham. Very little equipment is required: just a large, lidded container, and perhaps a meat slicer if you choose to make your own bacon.

A word of caution

You must pay particular attention to hygiene when home curing. In a properly cured piece of meat, the concentration of salt prohibits the growth of most microbes, but if the curing process is not thorough, or the level of salt is not high enough, the meat will spoil. For that reason, always ensure your hands are very clean or wear disposable gloves when handling the meat, and use a sterilising agent to clean plastic containers for storing brine. It is also a good idea to take advantage of modern technology and freeze the meat after curing it, until it is required. If at any time the meat smells bad, or mould begins to grow on the surface, it has been contaminated and should be discarded. Take no risks.

Cooking Techniques

Braising

This is the process of submerging meat in water, stock or a mixture of these, with alcohol, such as wine or beer, and some vegetables and herbs. The meat is then cooked slowly until it breaks down to a soft, sticky, melt-in-the-mouth consistency. Braising is good for using certain cuts of meat that, though flavourful, would be very tough if cooked any other way. Sometimes the meat is browned by frying it before braising to add flavour and colour. Cuts suitable for braising include shin, flank, oxtail, shortribs, pork belly, pork shoulder, beef cheeks, lamb and mutton breast and shoulder.

Frying

This is a quick method for browning the surface of meat by cooking it at a high temperature in fat. When frying it is important not to crowd too much meat into the pan all at once, otherwise it will not fry but stew and turn grey rather than browning properly. All cuts of steak are suitable for frying. They should then be left to rest before serving, to allow the temperature inside to equalise so that the juices remain in the meat and do not run out when it is sliced. In some cases, meat is fried first to add flavour and colour before being braised, roasted or pot roasted. This method is often called 'sealing'.

Oven roasting

Larger joints of meat are wonderful roasted in the oven. The meat is put into a hot oven initially to ensure that it browns and begins to cook quickly, then the heat is reduced until the joint cooks through. The lower the temperature at which this second cooking takes place, the more evenly the joint will cook, so temperatures between 120°C and 160°C are suitable for this second phase. Sirloin or rib of beef, legs, shoulder and loin of lamb, mutton or pork all make good roasts.

Pot roasting

In this method meat is usually browned well in hot fat then placed in a covered pot with aromatics, vegetables and a little stock or wine. This creates a humid environment to ensure that the meat doesn't dry out while it is cooking. It is a good method for cooking a joint that is to be eaten rare, such as a joint of top rump, or for a cut of meat that requires slower cooking, such as a rolled shoulder of lamb, or a whole tied shin. Other meats that suit roasting in a pot are topside and silverside of beef, and griskin (the lean part of a pork loin) and shoulder of pork.

Grilling

You can grill meat under hot grill elements in an oven or over coals on a barbecue, though the meat first needs to be oiled a little in order for it to brown. Placing the meat on to a grill rack allows the fat to drip off while it is cooking, making it a healthy, as well as delicious, way to cook meat. Smaller cuts of meat such as steaks and cutlets, and kebabs are good for grilling.

A note on cooking times

Mrs Beeton would not have had a temperature probe. Instead, she would have calculated cooking times according to the weight of the meat, and known her recipes and her equipment well. Today, however, we enjoy a greater variety of dishes, often use recipes or cuts of meat that we haven't tried before, and many of us are less at one with our cookers. We can still use the weight of the meat and the oven temperature as a good guide, but in order to get perfect results every time – especially with a new recipe or in an unfamiliar kitchen – it is well worth investing a few pounds in a temperature probe. Some thermometers even have alarms that sound when your meat reaches your chosen temperature.

It will take a bit of experimentation with cooking meat to different internal temperatures and resting joints for different amounts of time to thoroughly understand how the changes you make affect the final result, but you should find that even the first time you use a temperature probe the results will be more accurate than if you were using old-fashioned methods alone.

All of the recipes in this book are perfectly manageable without a temperature probe, but you might find yourself having to cut into a piece of meat to check that it's cooked through, rather than having the confidence to assume that it is. The table on the next page is a quick guide to cooking times by weight (the old-fashioned way) as well as by internal temperature.

Before cooking, remove the meat from the fridge and allow it to come to room temperature (about 15°C) for a couple of hours, uncovered. Beef and lamb can both be eaten rare to well done, while pork is traditionally served well done as it can contain a harmful parasite, trichinosis, if not cooked through – though cases of the disease today are rare. Pork cooked to an internal temperature of 70°C or showing no signs of pinkness at its centre is safe to eat.

Internal temperatures and cooking times

In order to achieve the correct final internal temperature, weigh the meat first and calculate the cooking time. Start from an initial oven temperature of 200–220°C. After 30 minutes, lower the temperature to 140–160°C for the remainder of the cooking time. Use the table below to calculate the total cooking time for your meat.

	Cooking time per 500g	Internal temperature
Rare beef and lamb	10–12 minutes	50–55°C
Medium beef and lamb	15 minutes	55–60°C
Well done pork, beef and lamb	20 minutes	70°C

Resting

Meat cooks from the outside inwards, which means that when a joint is removed from the oven, the outer layers will be hotter than the core. For the best results, remove the meat from the oven when the internal temperature is still a little short of the temperature you are aiming for. Resting the meat, covered loosely in foil in a warm place, allows the heat to equalise (spread from the outside to the centre). In a large joint, the temperature at the centre can rise by as much as 10°C while it is resting.

Carving

Loin

To carve a piece of loin on the bone, first remove the meat from the bones. Place the meat on a board, resting on its edge with the ribs uppermost, as shown in the illustration. Make a cut along the ribs, keeping your knife as close to the bone as possible.

Cut down to the base of the ribs, then turn your knife and slice along the base of the loin to remove it from the backbone.

Once the bones have been removed, you can cut down through the loin, producing neat slices.

When carving a piece of rolled loin or sirloin, there are no bones to remove. You can simply cut through the piece, slicing it into even, thick slices.

Fore rib

When you carve a piece of forerib, let the joint sit on its ribs – it will be more stable this way. First slice into the joint horizontally, between the meat and the rib bones. This can be done a little at a time – just enough to allow you to cut a few slices. If you cut too far, the meat will slide around while you are carving it.

Next, cut vertically into the meat, carving it into thick, even slices, which should come cleanly away from the bones.

Continue to cut horizontally and then vertically until you have cut the required amount of meat.

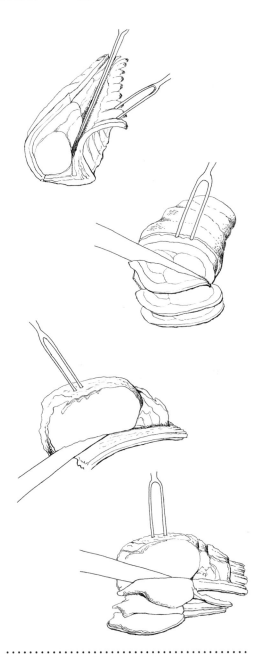

COLD
MEATS

SCOTCH EGGS

✱ Makes 4 ✱ Preparation time 20–30 minutes ✱ Cooking time 10–12 minutes

When Mrs Beeton was writing, Scotch eggs were usually eaten hot and served with gravy. Freshly made Scotch eggs are deliciously crisp and savoury and well worth a try, but you can enjoy these cold too, of course. If you are using a large pan rather than a deep-fryer to make these, only fill the pan a third full with oil and don't leave it unattended for a minute.

4 medium eggs

400g sausage meat

30g flour

4 tbsp milk

80g fine breadcrumbs from a stale loaf

vegetable oil, for frying

salt and freshly ground black pepper

special equipment

a deep-fryer and a temperature probe

Bring a pan of water to a steady simmer, then add the eggs. Cook them for 7 minutes over a medium heat, then drain and place in a bowl of iced water for 5 minutes. Cool completely and peel carefully under cold water. Then set the eggs aside.

Season the sausage meat well with salt and black pepper and divide it into 4 equal portions. Using wet hands, flatten each piece then shape into a cup big enough to hold an egg. Place an egg into each cup and then pinch the meat around the egg to seal it inside. Set aside on a plate.

Line a plate with non-stick baking paper and set aside. Prepare the coating for the eggs by placing the flour on a flat dish and seasoning it with salt and black pepper. Then, in a wide, shallow bowl beat the remaining egg with the milk and, finally, spread the breadcrumbs on a plate.

Take a meat-wrapped egg and roll it in the seasoned flour to coat, shaking off the excess. Now dip it in the beaten egg mixture, and then roll it in the breadcrumbs. Set aside on the plate lined with non-stick paper and repeat with the remaining eggs.

Preheat the oil in a deep-fryer to 160°C and when it is ready fry 2 eggs at a time for 6 minutes. Using long-handled tongs, turn the eggs 3–4 times to ensure they brown evenly. Once they are cooked, drain the first 2 eggs on a plate lined with kitchen paper while you make the other 2. Cool a little before serving. If you are not serving them right away, chill the Scotch eggs in an airtight container and eat within 2 days.

CORNISH PASTIES

✳ Makes 8 pasties ✳ Preparation time 35 minutes plus 1 hour chilling time ✳ Cooking time 40 minutes

A traditional Cornish pasty has a nice thick rim of pleated pastry, to be used as a handle for the hungry diner. You can crimp your pasties in the traditional way, as shown in the illustration, or simply press the two halves together firmly. Just make sure that none of the delicious filling escapes. Mrs Beeton gives an unusual recipe for a pasty using just meat and potato, but onions and swede have been added here to give the more familiar Cornish pasty flavour. Use skirt steak: it is inexpensive and easily procured from a good butcher.

for the pastry

500g plain flour, plus extra for dusting

1 tsp salt

125g suet

125g lard

for the filling

300g lean beef skirt, finely chopped

150g potato, peeled and grated

150g onions, peeled and grated

150g swede, peeled and grated

1½ tsp freshly ground black pepper

1½ tsp salt

1 egg, beaten, for brushing

special equipment

a 17cm round saucer to use as a template

To make the pastry, place the flour, salt, and half the suet in the bowl of a food processor and blend until fine. Then add the lard and blitz again until it is fully incorporated. Place the mixture into a bowl and add the rest of the suet, stirring well.

Add 120–150ml cold water and mix with a large fork until the dough begins to come together, adding a little more water if required. Pinch the pastry together with your fingertips until it forms a dough, then roll into a ball, wrap in cling film and chill. Meanwhile, add the beef and vegetables to a bowl. Sprinkle over the black pepper and stir together until fully combined.

Preheat the oven to 200°C/gas mark 6.

After the dough has been chilling for 1 hour, dust your work surface with some flour. Uncover the dough and roll it approximately 3–5mm thick, then cut out eight 17cm discs. You may need to re-roll the trimmings to cut the last 2 discs. Roll each disc into a slightly oval shape.

Now sprinkle the salt over the meat mixture, combine thoroughly and divide into 8 equal balls, placing one in the middle of each pastry oval.

Wet the edge of the pastry on one side of each oval with water. Fold the dry side up over the meat and, ensuring that no air has been trapped inside, press the edges well together to seal the pastry snugly round the filling.

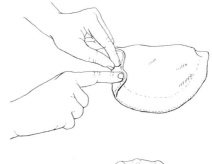

Crimp round the edge to perfect the seal, as shown in the illustrations (right). The finished pasty should have a D-shape.

Brush the beaten egg over the surface of the pasties, arrange them on a baking sheet lined with non-stick baking paper and place in the oven. After 10 minutes, turn the oven down to 160°C/gas mark 3 and bake for a further 30 minutes, or until the pasties are well browned and crisp. Remove from the oven and leave to cool on a wire rack for a few minutes before serving. These can be wrapped in foil and kept in the fridge for up to 4 days.

PORK PIES

✳ Serves 12 ✳ Preparation time 1 hour ✳ Cooking time 1 hour 30 minutes

For anyone fond of a slice of pork pie, making your own is a very worthwhile treat. Make these 1–2 days before eating and don't worry about finding proper pork pie tins – they are just as tasty made in deep cake tins with thin walls.

for the pastry

850g plain flour

15g salt

430ml water

240g lard, plus
extra for greasing

1 egg yolk

1 tbsp milk

for the pie filling

1.75kg pork mince, ideally
half shoulder and half belly
from a free-range pig

250g dry-cure bacon,
chopped small

6g ground white pepper

20g salt

8g ground mace

for the jelly

3 leaves gelatine

500ml pork or light chicken
stock (see page 69)

special equipment

2 x 17cm pork pie tins
or cake tins and a
temperature probe

Make the pastry

Sift the flour and salt together in a large bowl and set aside. Place the water and lard into a pan over a medium heat and bring to a gentle simmer. Remove from the heat and stir the liquid into the flour mixture using a large fork to blend thoroughly. Pour the mixture onto a work surface and mix with your hands to bring it together into a smooth ball, working carefully as the mixture will be hot. Cover the pastry with an inverted bowl and leave it to cool further for 5 minutes before using.

Meanwhile, preheat the oven to 200°C/gas mark 6. Grease the tins with a little lard or butter and line the base of each with non-stick baking paper.

Line the tins while the pastry is still warm and malleable. You will need one-quarter of the pastry for the lids, rolled out into two 17cm circles. Roll the remainder, for the pie bases and sides, into two 35cm circles and then use these to line the tins, pressing the pastry right into the corners and making sure there are no gaps. Leave an overhang of 2cm for sealing the lids.

Make the filling

Place the pork mince, bacon, white pepper, salt and mace into a bowl and mix it well together. Then divide the mixture between the 2 pastry-lined tins.

Wet the edges of the lids with water and place on top of the meat, pushing the circles right to the edges of the meat.

Fold the overhanging pastry over the lids and crimp these well together. Make a hole in centre of each lid and insert a rolled-up piece of foil to make a chimney for steam to escape through.

Whisk the egg yolk and milk together and brush the tops of the pies with the mixture, then place them in the oven. After 1 hour turn the heat down to 160°C/gas mark 3. Do not worry if the pies begin to weep, simply wipe the liquid away. After a further 30 minutes the pies should be a rich, golden-brown colour. Insert a temperature probe into the centre of one of the pies and if it reads 85°C the pies are cooked.

Transfer to a wire rack to cool and carefully remove the foil chimneys.

Make the jelly

While the pies are cooling, soak the gelatine leaves in a small bowl of cold water for 10 minutes. Place the stock in a saucepan over medium heat. When the gelatine leaves are ready, squeeze them to get rid of any excess water and add them to the stock, stirring to dissolve.

Pour half the stock (about 250ml) slowly and gently through the hole in the lid of one of the pies, then repeat with the second pie. The liquid will find its way between the pastry and meat and set as the pie cools.

Leave the pies in their tins until they are completely cold, then turn them out and store in a cool place wrapped in foil for 1–2 days before serving. They will keep like this for up to 1 week.

The Humble Pie

Mrs Beeton made raised pies using various different meats, but the humble pork pie is the one that has stood the test of time. The jelly, added after the pies are cooked, was originally a thick jellied stock, but dark pork or chicken stock combined with gelatine ensures a firm set.

POTTED BEEF

✳ Serves 4–6 as a starter ✳ Preparation time 30 minutes ✳ Cooking time 10 minutes

This smooth, buttery paste is flavoured with mace and cayenne pepper to give a bit of bite. Mrs Beeton recommends using the trimmed outer slices of roast beef for this recipe, which she then stores for some time. Today, we tend to make potted meats to eat within a few days, so I have added some shallot and ginger to lighten the mixture somewhat. If you intend to keep the meat for more than a week, it is best stored in the freezer. This recipe works equally well with the same quantity of venison or pork.

100g unsalted butter

500g cooked beef

½–1 tsp ground mace

½ tsp cayenne pepper

4 shallots, peeled and chopped

50g root ginger,
peeled and sliced

50g clarified butter
(see glossary)

salt and freshly ground
black pepper

special equipment

4–6 ramekins, one per diner

Trim the cooked meat, removing any sinews or blood vessels. Place the butter in a saucepan over a very low heat, add the vegetables and spices and let them stew for 10 minutes, or until soft and coloured but not browned.

Place the meat in a food processor and pour in the butter from the pan, keeping back all but 1 tbsp of the shallots. Blend the mixture thoroughly, season assertively with salt and black pepper, then press into ramekins. Seal the pots with clarified butter, cover with cling film and refrigerate.

Potted meat should be used within one week. It can be served as a starter with a sharp fruit jelly such as apple (see page 77) or redcurrant, and crusty bread.

SAUSAGE ROLLS

✲ Makes approx 20 mini sausage rolls or 10 larger ones (and 2kg puff pastry) ✲ Preparation time 30 minutes (plus 20 minutes of rolling, over 3 hours, if you are making your own puff pastry) ✲ Cooking time 15–20 minutes

A Mrs Beeton classic, this recipe is unchanged from the original except for the addition of a little cream to the egg yolk, giving the finished rolls a pleasing shine. You can, of course, make your sausage rolls with shop-bought puff pastry, but if you want to eat the best, it is very easy to make your own pastry. You only need 500g for Mrs Beeton's sausage rolls, but it is most convenient to make a good batch of puff pastry and freeze the rest for later. Sausage rolls make a great lunch served with fine English ale.

for the pastry	for the sausage rolls
1kg strong plain flour, plus extra for dusting	plain flour, for dusting
2 tsp salt	500g sausage meat
1kg cold unsalted butter	1 tbsp chopped herbs of your choice (optional)
1 tsp lemon juice	large pinch salt
500ml cold water	1 egg yolk
	1 tsp single cream

Make the pastry

Using a food processor, place all the flour with the salt and 250g of the butter, cut into cubes, into the bowl and pulse until the mixture resembles fine breadcrumbs. Pour this into a large bowl.

Add the lemon juice to the water and add two-thirds of the liquid to the bowl. Blend well with a fork, stirring quickly but gently. Using your fingertips, bring the dough together. Add more water as necessary until everything is evenly mixed and there are no dry lumps, then bring together into a smooth, supple lump. Form it into a flattened ball, wrap in cling film and chill for at least 1 hour.

Roll the remaining butter between 2 sheets of non-stick baking paper into an 18cm square that is 2.5cm thick. Lightly flour your work surface, then remove the dough from the fridge and unwrap. Place on the lightly floured surface and cut a deep cross in the dough, cutting about two-thirds of the way through to the work surface. Dust the ball with flour and fold the four segments out into a rough square shape. Dust this lightly with flour and roll it into a square about 28cm across, or large enough to take the block of butter set at a 45° angle.

Using a clean pastry brush, dust the pastry free of flour, place the butter in the centre at a 45° angle to the pastry and fold each corner of the pastry over the butter, pinching the dough together to seal any holes. Turn the dough over, dusting the work surface again with a little flour, and roll the pastry out into a 20 x 60cm rectangle. If the pastry sticks to the work surface dust it with a little more flour as required.

Once you have a rectangle of the right size, brush the pastry to remove any excess flour. Fold the third of the pastry nearest to you over the middle third, then fold in the top third on top of that so that you have a 20 x 20cm square and press, keeping the dough as square and even as you can. Place it on a plate in a cool place or the fridge to rest.

After 15 minutes remove the dough from the fridge and place so that the top open fold is on your left. Roll out again to 20 x 60cm and repeat the action above. Do this a total of 6 times, allowing the dough to rest in between each fold. After resting it for the last time, roll the pastry into a 30 x 20cm rectangle. Cut this evenly into 4 parts. One part (500g) will do for the sausage rolls. Wrap the 3 other portions tightly in cling film, then seal in foil and freeze.

Make the sausage rolls

When you are ready to start the sausage rolls, preheat the oven to 200°C/gas mark 6 and line a baking tray with non-stick baking parchment. Dust your work surface with a little flour. Divide your 500g puff pastry in half and roll each piece out into a 14 x 44cm rectangle.

Mix the sausage meat with the herbs, if using, and salt, then divide the mixture in half and roll each piece into a sausage shape 44cm long. Place the sausage meat on the rolled-out pastry, leaving 2cm bare along one long edge where the pastry will join. Fold the pastry over the meat to make a long roll, ensuring that no air is trapped inside. Whisk the egg yolk and cream together and brush the mixture over the inside edges, then pinch together to form a good seal, pressing down with a fork, and trim off any surplus, leaving a neat 1cm join to one side of the roll.

Brush all over the surface with the egg wash, then, using a sharp knife, divide the sausage roll crossways into either 10 large sausage rolls or 20 smaller ones. Arrange the sausage rolls on the prepared baking tray and place in the oven. If you are making mini sausage rolls, bake them for 15–20 minutes. The larger sausage rolls need 20 minutes in the oven, and then a further 10 minutes at 180°C/gas mark 4 to ensure the pastry is cooked through.

Leave to cool slightly before serving or eat cold. These can be wrapped in foil and kept in the fridge for up to 4–5 days.

ROASTING

'Beef is the foundation of stock, gravies, braises, etc; its nutritious and succulent gravy gives body and flavour to numberless ragouts. It is an exhaustive mine in the hands of a skilful artist, and is truly the king of the kitchen. Without it, no soup, no gravy; and its absence would produce almost a famine in the civilised world!'

Beeton's Book of Household Management

ROAST FORE RIB OF BEEF

✳ Serves 6–8 ✳ Preparation time 5 minutes ✳ Cooking time 1 hour 30 minutes plus 30 minutes resting time

Mrs Beeton notes that 'the fore-rib is considered the primest roasting piece' and that 'a Yorkshire pudding ... will be considered an agreeable addition'. As always with roast beef, she also recommends a garnish of horseradish. This joint is perfect for roasting as the fat from the rib bastes the meat as it cooks. Ask your butcher to cut through the base of the ribs to make the joint easier to carve once it has been cooked.

3.5kg joint beef fore rib on the bone

2 onions, peeled and chopped

1 carrot, peeled and chopped

1 stick celery, trimmed and chopped

200ml light red wine

1 large thyme sprig

500ml jellied beef stock (see page 70)

10g unsalted butter

10g flour (optional)

salt and freshly ground black pepper

special equipment

a roasting tin and a temperature probe

Preheat the oven to 230°C/gas mark 8. Sprinkle the meat with 1 tsp salt and some freshly ground black pepper, rubbing it into the cut sides of the meat and the fat. Put the vegetables in a roasting tin, set the beef on top and place the tin in the hot oven. After 30 minutes turn the heat down to 140°C/gas mark 1.

For a rare joint, cook for a further 45 minutes to 1 hour at the lower temperature – it is ready when the internal temperature reaches 45°C. Remove the joint from the oven, wrap it well in foil and leave it in a warm place to rest for 30 minutes. The internal temperature should rise another 10°C during the resting time. For a medium joint, cook at the lower temperature for 1½ hours or until a temperature probe inserted into the meat reads 50–55°C, then remove from the oven and rest as above.

While the meat rests, make the gravy. Remove and discard the vegetables from the roasting tin and pour away the fat. Add the red wine and place the tin over a medium heat to reduce, stirring to scrape up any sediment from the bottom of the tin. Once the wine is reduced, add the thyme and stock, bring to a simmer and whisk in the butter. The jellied stock gives a light, syrupy gravy. If you prefer it thicker, mash 10g flour with the butter before adding it to the pan. Simmer for 3 minutes and then strain the gravy into a warmed sauceboat.

Serve thin slices of the meat with roast potatoes, steamed cabbage and Yorkshire puddings (see page 89).

RUMP STEAK

✳ Serves 4 ✳ Preparation time 5 minutes ✳ Cooking time 20–25 minutes

Rump steak is made up from several different muscles, each with a different texture – and the flavour is superb. Mrs Beeton comments that rump can be less tender than fillet or sirloin, but by cooking the steak in a large piece and resting it, you maximise the tenderness and get all of the super flavour that rump has to offer.

2 tbsp light olive oil

1kg rump steak, no more than 4cm thick, tied in one large piece

salt and freshly ground black pepper

10g unsalted butter

1 large shallot, finely chopped

1 tsp fresh thyme leaves

50ml light red wine

100ml jellied beef or dark chicken stock (see page 70 or 68)

special equipment

a roasting tin and a temperature probe

Preheat the oven to 200°C/gas mark 6.

Place a large frying pan over a medium to high heat. Add the oil, then the steak. Fry for 3 minutes then turn and fry the other side for 3 minutes, seasoning with a little salt and pepper as it cooks. If the steak begins to lift up from the pan, press it down with a fish slice so that it colours evenly. Transfer the steak to the roasting tin and save any excess fat from the pan for finishing the sauce later.

Place the roasting tin in the oven. For a rare steak, roast for 10–12 minutes, or until a temperature probe inserted in the meat reads 45–50°C. For a medium steak, roast for 15–18 minutes, or until a temperature probe inserted in the meat reads 50–55°C. Remove from the oven, wrap the steak in foil and leave to rest in a warm place for 10 minutes.

Meanwhile, melt the butter in the frying pan over a medium heat and add the shallot. Cook, stirring, until the shallot is softening and beginning to brown at the edges. Add the thyme leaves and stir in the red wine. Simmer until the wine has reduced, then add the stock. Simmer and reduce again until the sauce has a syrupy consistency. Unwrap the steak and pour any juices left behind in the foil back into the pan with the sauce and stir them in. Pour the sauce into a jug or sauceboat. Place the steak on a warmed serving dish and take it to the table. Carve it on the bias, placing slices onto diners' plates and passing round the sauce. Serve with potatoes, grilled mushrooms and parsley & garlic butter (see page 82).

POT-ROAST TOP RUMP

✳ Serves 6 ✳ Preparation time 20 minutes ✳ Cooking time 1 hour 30 minutes

This is a super way of maximising the flavour of a piece of beef. Ask your butcher to cut you a piece of top rump or the corner end of the silverside and tie it to keep its shape during cooking. Mrs Beeton tended to cook her stewed or braised beef for many hours, but a top rump can be pot roasted and eaten medium and it will be delicious.

1.5kg top rump, tied

5g Maldon or other flaky sea salt

1 stick celery, trimmed and cut into 3cm chunks

2 carrots, peeled and cut into 3cm chunks

2 onions, peeled and cut into large chunks

3 bay leaves

bunch fresh thyme

¼ tsp freshly ground black pepper

150ml jellied beef stock (see page 70)

300ml white wine

special equipment

a large flameproof casserole with a lid and a temperature probe

Preheat the oven to 160°C/gas mark 3.

Place a large frying pan over a low–medium heat. Put the rump fat-side down in the pan and allow the fat to render for 10 minutes, or until the meat is golden brown. Then turn the heat up high and brown the meat well on all sides, adding a little of the salt and turning frequently until it is a rich, dark brown all over. Remove from the pan and set aside to rest.

Place the vegetables and all the remaining ingredients into the large casserole and place over a medium to high heat. When the mixture is boiling, set the meat on top of the vegetables and cover with a lid. For medium-rare, cook the meat in the oven for 30 minutes or until a temperature probe inserted into the centre reads 50°C, then remove from the oven and set aside to rest with the lid slightly open. If you prefer your meat medium to well done, increase the cooking time to 45 minutes or until the temperature reads 60°C before resting as above.

After 20–30 minutes' resting time, carve the meat and arrange it on a large, warmed serving dish with the vegetables. Pour the pan juices into a serving jug and offer alongside the meat. Serve with a potato and cream gratin and a green salad.

Note: If you have any leftover beef, serve cold slices for lunch or in sandwiches, or use it to make potted beef (see page 25).

ROAST LOIN OF PORK

✱ Serves 8 ✱ Preparation time 10 minutes ✱ Cooking time 1–2 hours plus 30 minutes resting time

A loin of pork is pure carnivore indulgence – moist and succulent inside and crispy outside. Ask your butcher to cut you a piece of loin on the bone, and then to cut through the backbone so that you can carve the loin into chops at home once it is cooked. Also ask to have the pork skin scored for crackling. When you get home, remove the pork from its wrapping and place, uncovered, on a tray in the fridge to allow the skin to dry well. This helps the crackling form.

2.5kg loin of free-range pork with 8 ribs

1 tbsp sunflower oil

fine salt and freshly ground black pepper

special equipment

a large roasting tin and a temperature probe

Preheat the oven to 220°C/gas mark 7.

Place the pork, skin-side up, in a large roasting tin. Ensure that the skin is completely dry, then brush with the oil and sprinkle all over with salt. Roast for 40 minutes to crackle the skin then reduce the heat to 140°C/gas mark 1 for a further hour. At this point a temperature probe inserted into the middle of the pork should read at least 60°C. If it does not, leave the meat in the oven for a further 20 minutes, then retest.

When it has cooked, remove the pork from the oven. Cover with foil and leave to rest in a warm place for at least 40 minutes. If the skin is not crackly all over, place it under a medium to hot grill until it crisps up, but be careful not to let it burn.

When you are ready to serve, transfer the pork to a chopping board and carve into thick slices, down through the line of the chops, giving a chop to each person. This is delicious served with apple sauce (see page 78) and potato and cream gratin.

ROAST SHOULDER OF PORK

✲ Serves 6–8 ✲ Preparation time 15 minutes ✲ Cooking time 3 hours plus 30 minutes resting

Although Mrs Beeton featured several pork roasts, shoulder wasn't one of them. However, this is a good joint to try if you are new to the kitchen. It is very forgiving as it has a number of small muscles interwoven with a little fat, which helps keep it moist. It is also a very economical cut of meat. To keep the dish true to Mrs Beeton it is roasted with sage and served with a modern interpretation of her apple sauce: a cider gravy.

2.5kg rolled shoulder joint of free-range or rare-breed pork

salt and freshly ground black pepper

2 sticks celery, trimmed and cut into chunks

2 onions, peeled and cut into chunks

1 carrot, peeled and cut into chunks

4 sage leaves

125ml medium dry cider

500ml light chicken or pork stock (see page 69)

10g unsalted butter (optional)

10g plain flour (optional)

special equipment

a roasting tin

Preheat the oven to 220°C/gas mark 7.

Ensure that the pork skin is well dried, then season lightly all over with salt and black pepper. Place the vegetables and sage into a roasting tin and set the pork on top. Roast for 30 mins, or until the fat starts to render and the skin starts to crackle.

Reduce the heat to 140°C/gas mark 1 and cook for a further 2½ hours. After this time the pork will be fully cooked through. Remove the meat to a warmed serving dish, cover with foil and leave in a warm place for at least 30 minutes while you finish the sauce.

Pour any excess fat from the roasting tin (you can reserve this for another dish) and place the tin over a medium heat. Add the cider and, using a wooden spatula, scrape up any the caramelised bits, dissolving them in the liquid. Simmer until the cider has reduced by half. Add the stock and reduce a little more. Season the sauce to taste with a little salt and a grinding of black pepper.

If you like a thicker sauce, mash 10g unsalted butter with 10g plain flour and whisk it into the sauce then simmer for 3 minutes to thicken. Strain the sauce into a hot sauceboat.

If your pork skin has not crackled well, preheat the grill to high. Put the pork joint, skin-side up, under the grill until it is crisp and brown all over, turning it with a pair of tongs. Be careful not to burn the skin. Serve the pork sliced and accompanied by braised red cabbage and puy lentils.

ROAST LEG OF MUTTON

✳ Serves 6–8 ✳ Preparation time 5 minutes ✳ Cooking time 1 hour 30 minutes plus 45 minutes resting time

The ingredients for this recipe haven't changed in 150 years – all that is really needed is a leg of mutton and a little salt to enhance the flavour of the meat. Mrs Beeton roasted the meat in front of the fire, basting it continually, but today it's a far less labour-intensive process. Use a leg of Herdwick or Manx Loaghtan mutton if you can, for its rich and nutty flavour. Two of the best producers in the UK are listed at the back of the book.

2.7kg leg of mutton, H-bone removed

salt and freshly ground black pepper

special equipment

a roasting tin and a temperature probe

If you are unsure about doing it yourself, ask your butcher to remove the H-bone to make carving easier. Preheat the oven to 220°C/gas mark 7.

Season the leg all over with 1 tsp salt and a few grindings of black pepper and place it in a roasting tin. Roast for 30 minutes then turn the heat down to 140°C/gas mark 1. For medium to medium-rare meat, cook for a further 45 minutes, or until a temperature probe inserted to the thickest part of the leg reads 50°C, before removing. If you prefer your meat medium to well done, cook for an additional 25 minutes, or until a temperature probe inserted to the thickest part of the leg reads 60°C.

Remove the meat from the oven, cover with foil and put in a warm place to rest for up to 45 minutes before slicing. Serve this dish with haricot beans and some spinach cooked with a little butter, garlic and nutmeg.

SLOW
COOKING

BRAISED SHORTRIBS OF BEEF

✱ Serves 4 ✱ Preparation time 45 minutes ✱ Cooking time 9–10 hours in a slow cooker or 5–6 hours in the oven

Shortribs, sometimes also called boiling beef ribs or rising rib, are a very inexpensive cut of meat. They are popular in Scotland, but often overlooked elsewhere – which is a shame as they have a delicious flavour and texture. Mrs Beeton cooked shortribs plainly with water, which makes for a good, gelatinous stew, but the addition of vegetables, herbs and ale gives a richer, more generous one-pot meal that is perfect for a winter weekend supper.

1.7kg shortribs, cut into
8 x 10cm pieces

2 onions, peeled and
thickly sliced

2 carrots, peeled and cut
into 2.5cm chunks

2 sticks celery, trimmed
and cut into 2.5cm chunks

500ml medium-strength
dark ale

250ml jellied beef stock
(see page 70)

1 garlic clove, peeled
and left whole

1 large thyme sprig

1 bay leaf

4 carrots, peeled and cut
into 8cm lengths

special equipment

a large roasting tin and a
flameproof casserole dish or 3-litre
slow cooker

Preheat the oven to 220°C/gas mark 7. Arrange the shortribs in a large roasting tin, leaving plenty of space between them. Roast for 30 minutes, or until well browned.

Remove to the casserole dish or slow cooker. Add the onion, carrot chunks and celery to the roasting tin and toss them in the dripping that has come from the ribs. Roast for 10–15 minutes, or until browned. Pour off the excess fat and reserve it for another dish.

Add the cooked vegetables to the ribs along with the ale, stock, garlic, thyme and bay leaf. Either slow cook for 9–10 hours on a low heat or put in the oven at 140°C/gas mark 1 for 5–6 hours. An hour before serving, add the second quantity of carrots and cook until both they and the meat are tender.

BRAISED OX CHEEKS

✳ Serves 4 ✳ Preparation time 30minutes ✳ Cooking time 3-4 hours

It is typical of Mrs Beeton to include a recipe for an extremely economical cut of beef and yet make something of it fit to grace any table. The ingredients have been adjusted here to substitute easily available ingredients as well as to refine the flavours for the modern palate, but the net result is true to the original. Try these beef cheeks for a family dinner. They have a distinctive, rich taste and offer great value for money. Ask your butcher to trim them for you to remove any sinew and fat.

2 tbsp light olive oil

2 boned beef cheeks, trimmed

1 onion, peeled and cut into large chunks

1 carrot, peeled and cut into large chunks

1 stick celery, trimmed and cut into large chunks

1 small leek, cut in half lengthways and then into chunks

6 cherry tomatoes or 1 tbsp tomato purée

500ml red wine

350ml jellied beef stock (see page 70)

2 bay leaves

few thyme sprigs

2 garlic cloves, peeled

8 allspice berries

2 cloves

salt and freshly ground black pepper

special equipment

a flameproof casserole dish with a lid

Preheat the oven to 140°C/gas mark 1.

Heat a large frying pan over a high heat and add half the olive oil. Season the cheeks with ½ tsp salt and add them to the pan. Brown the cheeks well on all sides then remove them to a plate. Lower the heat under the pan to medium, add the other half of the oil and fry the onion, carrot, celery and leek until well coloured, then add the tomatoes or tomato purée and cook until the mixture is thick and starting to catch.

Transfer the vegetables to the plate with the beef. Remove the pan from the heat and add the wine, stirring to dissolve all of the sediment. Then arrange the beef and vegetables snugly in the casserole, pour the wine over the top and then add the stock, bay leaves, thyme, garlic and spices. Place the lid on the casserole and bake in the oven for 3-4 hours, until the meat is very tender.

Pour the liquid from the casserole through a fine sieve into a pan over a medium heat. The meat and vegetables should be left in the casserole, and kept warm. Skim any fat from the surface of the liquid with a large spoon and then simmer the mixture to reduce until you have a lovely rich sauce. Season with salt and black pepper. Carve the cheeks into thick slices and serve with the vegetables alongside, pouring the sauce back over the top.

BRAISED OXTAIL

✻ Serves 4 ✻ Preparation time 30 minutes ✻ Cooking time 4 hours–4 hours 30 minutes

This recipe tastes even better if you cook it a day ahead – which makes it ideal for serving to guests because all the work is done the day before, leaving you free to entertain. Mrs Beeton uses very traditional English seasonings in this dish, including mace, mushroom ketchup and cloves, to which I have added ale for a really meaty, savoury dish.

1 oxtail, weighing around 1.5kg, cut in slices

150g cured streaky bacon, diced

2 onions, peeled and chopped into chunks

500ml light beer

8 allspice berries

1 pinch ground mace

juice and zest of ½ lemon, plus extra juice to taste

30ml mushroom ketchup

2 cloves

350ml jellied beef or dark chicken stock (see page 70 or 68)

2 bay leaves

2 tbsp finely chopped parsley

salt and freshly ground black pepper

special equipment

a large roasting tin and a flameproof casserole with a lid

Ask your butcher to slice the oxtail for you if you are unsure about doing it yourself. Preheat the oven to 220°C/gas mark 7. Place the oxtail pieces in a large roasting tin, season with a pinch of salt and pepper, and scatter over the bacon. Roast for 30 minutes, until the meat is golden brown all over.

Pour off and discard most of the fat, then add the onions and return the tin to the oven. Cook, stirring occasionally, for 10–15 minutes, or until the onion begins to colour. Remove from the oven and reduce the heat to 160°C/gas mark 3.

Scrape the oxtail and onions from the roasting tin into the casserole. Pour half of the beer into the roasting tin and stir to dissolve any caramelised bits sticking to the bottom. Then pour this, along with all of the rest of the ingredients except the chopped parsley, into the casserole. Stir well, cover tightly with a lid or foil and place in the oven.

After 1 hour turn the meat to ensure it cooks evenly in the liquid. After 4 hours the meat should be very tender and sticky. If not, leave it in the oven for another 15–30 minutes.

Remove from the oven and pour the liquid into a large jug, discarding the bay leaves and leaving everything else behind in the casserole dish. Let the liquid settle in the jug and then use a ladle or large spoon to skim off and discard any fat that rises to the top. Taste the liquid and add a little salt, pepper and lemon juice if needed, then pour the sauce back over the meat and turn the pieces in it to moisten them. Stir through the chopped parsley then serve with parsnips and freshly boiled Savoy cabbage.

BREAST OF LAMB EPIGRAMMES

✻ Serves 4 ✻ Preparation time 20 minutes ✻ Cooking time 3 hours

Mrs Beeton originally intended this recipe for oxtail but the technique is now more commonly used with lamb. Belly of lamb, like oxtail, needs long, slow cooking to make the best of its tasty, soft meat. The second cooking in breadcrumbs adds a pleasing crunch to the final dish and shows that this usually fatty cut is capable of surprising delicacy.

700g belly of lamb, including bones

1 small carrot, peeled and cut into chunks

1 small onion, peeled and cut into chunks

1 stick celery, trimmed and cut into chunks

small bunch thyme

1 bay leaf

500ml light chicken or lamb stock (see page 69)

plain flour, for dusting

1 medium egg

3 tsp Dijon mustard

80g breadcrumbs

50g clarified butter (see glossary)

salt and freshly ground black pepper

special equipment

an ovenproof dish, a 20 x 10cm baking tray and a weight

Preheat the oven to 140°C/gas mark 1. Season the lamb with salt and pepper and place it into the ovenproof dish with the veg, thyme and bay leaf. Heat the stock over a medium heat and pour it over the lamb. Cover tightly with greaseproof paper and foil and braise in the oven for 3 hours, or until the meat is falling off the bones. Remove the lamb from the liquid using a slotted spoon or tongs and place it in a large bowl.

When it has cooled a little, strip the meat away from the bones and set it on a plate. You should have around 300g of meat. Discard the bones, skin and sinew, and season the meat with a large pinch of salt and a few grindings of black pepper. Drizzle over 2 tbsp of the cooking liquor.

Line the baking tray with cling film, leaving a long overhang on 2 sides, and press the meat into it to form a layer 1.5cm deep. Pull the cling film up and over the meat to make a tight parcel, press with a weight and chill until cold. The gelatine in the meat will cause it to set.

Meanwhile, preheat the oven to 200°C/gas mark 6. Put some flour on a plate and sprinkle over ½ tsp salt. Beat together the egg and mustard in a bowl and spread the breadcrumbs on another plate. When the meat is cold, cut it into 8 equal pieces. Dip each piece first into the seasoned flour, then into the egg mixture and finally into the breadcrumbs to coat.

Melt the butter over a high heat and fry the epigrammes on both sides until golden brown. Transfer to the oven for 10 minutes. Serve with Dijon mustard and a watercress salad.

STEAK & KIDNEY PUDDING

✳ Serves 4 ✳ Preparation time 45 minutes ✳ Cooking time 4 hours

The use of kidney in this steak pudding supplanted the traditional use of oysters as a filler in beef dishes. The original recipe came from a 'Sussex lady', who contributed it to the *English Woman's Domestic Magazine*, which Mrs Beeton edited. In this recipe, self-raising flour is used to make the pastry. This was not available to Mrs Beeton, but it lightens the resulting pastry considerably and also makes it more absorbent, which is excellent for puddings.

for the suet pastry

375g self-raising flour

scant 1 tsp salt

130g suet, grated

250ml cold water

for the filling

2 tbsp dripping or sunflower oil, plus extra for greasing

130g beef kidney, diced

600g chuck steak, cut into 2cm dice

1 onion, peeled and finely sliced

½ tbsp plain flour

1 heaped tsp thyme leaves

1 large bay leaf

2 tbsp Worcestershire sauce

2 tbsp mushroom ketchup

130ml stout

130ml jellied beef stock (see page 70)

salt and freshly ground black pepper

special equipment

a 1-litre pudding basin, a pastry cutter or muffin ring and a 4-litre saucepan

Sift the flour and salt into a large bowl and mix in the suet. Add half of the water. Stir well with a fork, working quickly but gently. Using your fingertips, bring the dough together. Add more water as necessary until everything is evenly mixed and there are no dry lumps of flour.

Bring the mixture together into a smooth, supple lump and leave it to rest for 10 minutes. Roll two-thirds for lining the pudding basin, and the remainder to make the lid. Set these on a plate, cover with cling film and chill until needed. Grease the pudding basin and set aside

Heat half the fat in a frying pan over a high heat and add the kidney. Brown it all over, then remove it from the pan and set aside. Add the remaining fat to the pan, then the steak and 1 tsp salt. Brown well, then add the onion, reduce the heat and cook for 10 minutes, or until the onion is soft. Sprinkle over the flour and add the thyme, bay leaf, Worcestershire sauce, mushroom ketchup and ½ tsp black pepper. Cook, stirring, for 5 minutes, ensuring the flour is well blended in. Return the kidney to the pan and add the stout and stock, then check the seasoning and remove from the heat.

Once the filling is cold, line the pudding basin with the suet pastry and pour the filling into the lined basin. If the filling is warm at this point it will melt the pastry and cause it to be tough. Dampen the edge of the pastry with a little water and place the pastry lid on top, crimping the edges well.

Pleat a large piece of greaseproof paper down the centre to allow room for expansion during steaming. Cover the top of the pudding with the pleated paper, then a pleated layer of foil, and secure with kitchen string around the edge of the basin, leaving some extra string to make a handle for lifting.

Set a pastry cutter or muffin ring in the base of a 4-litre saucepan and place the pudding basin on top. Pour boiling water around the pudding basin to a depth of 15cm. Cover with a lid and bring the water to a simmer, then reduce the heat and simmer for 4 hours, topping up with boiling water as necessary. Once cooked, invert the pudding onto a warmed seving dish and serve with steamed vegetables.

BRAISED MUTTON WITH BARLEY & MINT

✳ Serves 4 ✳ Preparation time 10 minutes ✳ Cooking time 3–4 hours

In this recipe, pearl barley has been used in place of the haricot beans Mrs Beeton specified, but if you prefer the original combination, use the haricot beans recipe in *Mrs Beeton Soups & Sides* and simply add the cooked beans to the roasting tin in place of the cooked barley, finishing the recipe in the same way. Save any leftovers for the leftover mutton broth on page 72.

2.7kg shoulder of mutton

2 onions, peeled and cut into large chunks

1 large carrot, peeled and cut into large chunks

2 sticks celery, trimmed and cut into large chunks

small bunch thyme

4 bay leaves

500ml dark chicken stock (see page 68)

200ml water

80g pearl barley

few mint sprigs, stems discarded and leaves chopped

salt and freshly ground black pepper

special equipment

a roasting tin

Preheat the oven to 220°C/gas mark 7.

Trim off and discard any excess fat from the shoulder, then place in a roasting tin and season with 1 teaspoon salt and a few grindings of black pepper.

Roast for 30 minutes, or until dark golden brown, then, remove from the oven and pour off any fat. Place the vegetables, thyme, 3 bay leaves, stock and water into the tin with the meat, cover tightly with greaseproof paper and foil and return to the oven at 140°C/gas mark 1 for 3½ hours, until the meat is very tender and falling off the bone.

When the mutton has gone back into the oven, cover the barley with water and leave it to soak. About 1 hour before the meat is ready, simmer the barley with the remaining bay leaf for about 30–40 minutes, or until cooked and tender. Strain it through a sieve, fish out and discard the bay leaf and set the barley aside until needed.

When the shoulder is ready, lift it out of the tin and place it on a warmed serving dish, cover loosely with foil and leave to rest. Meanwhile, pour the cooking liquid from the tin through a sieve into a large measuring jug. Skim and discard any fat that floats to the surface. Then return the liquid to the roasting tin with the vegetables. Add the strained barley and place over a medium heat. Warm through and check the seasoning. Fish out and discard the bay leaves then stir through the mint and serve with steamed green vegetables.

FAST
COOKING

'Few domestic animals are so profitable or so useful to man as the much maligned pig, and no other yields him a more varied or more luxurious repast ... for almost every part of the animal, either fresh, salted, or dried, is used for food; and even those viscera not so employed are of the utmost utility in a domestic point of view.'

Mrs Beeton's Book of Household Management

LIVER & BACON

✳ Serves 4 ✳ Preparation time 10 minutes ✳ Cooking time 25 minutes

Recommended by Mrs Beeton for its flavour and economy, liver has fallen out of favour in recent years. If you haven't cooked it before, this is a great way to enjoy it – roasted, then sliced to pink perfection. Free-range or rare-breed liver is the best, if you can find it.

8 rashers back or streaky bacon

600g thick lobe of free-range pig's liver, trimmed of any large tubes

2–3 tbsp sunflower oil or dripping

2 large or 3 medium onions, peeled and cut into 3mm slices

100ml dark chicken or jellied beef stock (see page 68 or 70)

6 sage leaves, sliced finely

salt and freshly ground black pepper

special equipment

a roasting tin and a temperature probe

Preheat the oven to 200°C/gas mark 6. Lay the bacon rashers in a roasting tin, ensuring they do not overlap, and set aside.

Rub the liver with 1 tbsp of the fat and season with salt and black pepper. Place a large frying pan over a medium to high heat and, when the pan is hot, add the liver. Cook, turning occasionally, until the liver is firm and evenly browned. Turn the heat off but keep the pan for cooking the onions. Place the liver in the roasting tin with the bacon and transfer to the oven. Remove the bacon after 12–15 minutes, drain any excess fat and keep warm on a plate. Then pierce the thickest part of the liver with a temperature probe. When it reads 50–55°C, or when the liver begins to be resistant to the tip of your finger, remove it from the oven and wrap closely with foil. Cover with a tea towel and set it aside to rest, keeping the probe in place to check that the temperature has risen to 60-65°C before serving. The liver will be evenly pink and medium. If you like well-done liver, cook it initially until it reaches 65°C, then leave it to rest.

Heat the remaining fat in the frying pan over a medium heat and add a pinch of salt. Add the onions and cook, stirring occasionally, for about 10 minutes, or until they soften and begin to brown. Add the stock and the sage, turn the heat down and simmer until the liquid has reduced to a sticky glaze.

Slice the liver into large, thin pieces. Serve with the bacon and onions on the side and a salad of ripe, sliced tomatoes and finely chopped red onion.

DEVILLED KIDNEYS

✴ Serves 4 ✴ Preparation time 15 minutes ✴ Cooking time 10 minutes

Mrs Beeton usually fried kidneys and served them simply on toast with lemon juice or gravy poured over. We still serve kidneys on toast today, but the accompanying sauce has been refined to a sharp, spicy mixture that provides an excellent foil to the richness of the kidneys. This devilled kidneys recipe is a modern classic. Ask your butcher to save you some fresh British lambs' kidneys. Avoid the vacuum-packed ones brought in from abroad as they are inferior.

1 tbsp sherry vinegar

1 tsp Worcestershire sauce

dash Tabasco sauce, to taste

2 tsp English mustard powder

8 lambs' kidneys

20g unsalted butter

60ml white wine

2 tbsp single cream

squeeze of lemon juice (optional)

small bunch parsley, stems discarded, leaves chopped

4 slices good bread, toasted and buttered, to serve

salt and freshly ground black pepper

In a bowl whisk together the vinegar, Worcestershire sauce, Tabasco and mustard powder (this is the devilling mixture) and set aside until needed. Now place the kidneys on their sides on a chopping board. Cut them in half horizontally and open them up to reveal a white core. Use a small knife to remove all of it, then cut each half kidney in half across to give 2 equal segments.

Place a frying pan over a high heat. When hot, add the butter, and then the kidneys. Fry for 4–5 minutes, or until they are browned on all sides. Remove the kidneys from the pan and set them aside. Reduce the heat to medium and stir the wine into the pan, scraping up the sediment to dissolve it.

When the wine has reduced by half, stir in the devilling mixture and cook for 1 minute, then add the cream and let it cook for another minute.

Remove from the heat, season with a good pinch of salt and a few grindings of black pepper. If you like, you can adjust the sharpness with a squeeze of fresh lemon juice. Sprinkle with chopped parsley and serve on hot buttered toast.

LAMB CHOPS BRAISED WITH SPRING VEGETABLES

✳ Serves 4 ✳ Preparation time 15 minutes ✳ Cooking time 25 minutes

Mrs Beeton recommends peas and asparagus as the 'favourite accompaniments of lamb chops', and this recipe provides a method for combining the three elements together in a simple one-pot dish. The lamb cooks quickly so cook the fat first to add flavour, before seasoning and browning the meat itself. This makes a quick and delicious midweek dinner.

8 lamb chops

150g podded baby broad beans

25g unsalted butter

4 spring onions, trimmed and cut into 10cm pieces

150g young peas

20 asparagus tips, cut in half

200ml dark chicken stock (see page 68)

small bunch parsley, large stalks removed, leaves finely chopped

zest of ½ lemon, finely grated

salt and freshly ground black pepper

Heat a frying pan large enough to take all the chops in a single layer over a low to medium heat.

Stand the chops up on their skin edges, side by side, and cook to render and brown the fat for 15 minutes, or until the fat is a deep golden brown. Alternatively, place the chops skin-side up in a roasting tin under a low to medium grill so that the fat browns and renders without shrinking. Whichever way you decide to do this, keep an eye on the chops to ensure that they do not burn.

While the fat renders, bring a small pan of water to a boil over a high heat and add a large pinch of salt. Add the broad beans and bring the water back to boiling. Let them cook for 1 minute and then drain and plunge them into a bowl of iced water. Peel off the skins and save the tiny green beans.

When the fat has rendered and you are ready to cook the lamb, season the chops on both sides with a pinch of salt and pepper and turn the heat under the frying pan to high. Brown the chops well on both sides and then set aside on a plate and cover loosely with foil.

Discard any fat from the pan, reduce the heat to medium and add the unsalted butter and the spring onions. Cook for one minute, stirring, and then add all of the vegetables and the stock. Turn the heat to high and simmer for one minute. Return the chops to the pan to heat through for 5 minutes. Turn them occasionally and allow the sauce to reduce a little. Before serving, sprinkle over the parsley and the lemon zest.

CURING

HUNTER'S SPICED BEEF

✳ Serves 8 ✳ Preparation time 30 minutes plus 5 days marinating and 2–3 days resting ✳ Cooking time 1 hour

This unusual recipe for a salted and spiced beef is truly excellent, but you do have to start it up to 10 days ahead of serving. Mrs Beeton used a round of beef, which is a huge cut, but this recipe uses a smaller joint known as the salmon cut of silverside. It is a very lean joint, containing hardly any fat, so it must only be cooked to medium to remain moist. To get nearer to the old-fashioned taste of beef, try to source an old-fashioned breed such as a Dexter, suppliers of which can be found at the back of the book.

50g soft brown sugar

20g Maldon sea salt
or other flaky sea salt

4 bay leaves

1 tsp allspice berries

1 tsp black peppercorns

1 tsp juniper berries

4 whole cloves

1kg piece salmon cut of silverside (beef), ideally from a Dexter animal (a small silverside from a Dexter animal will be roughly 8cm in diameter. If it is from a conventional animal it will be much thicker, and will need cutting into 2 even, thinner pieces)

1 tbsp sunflower oil

special equipment

a ceramic baking dish or stainless steel bowl, a roasting tin and a temperature probe

Mix the sugar, salt, bay leaves and all the spices together in a ceramic baking dish or stainless steel bowl. Add the beef and turn it in the spices to ensure it is evenly coated, rubbing the seasoning in well. Cover with cling film and refrigerate for 5 days, turning the meat over once a day. By the end of this time the beef will be firm and cured.

Remove the beef from the fridge and leave it to sit for 1–2 hours to come up to room temperature. Rinse off the spices under cold water and dry with a piece of kitchen paper.

Preheat the oven to 160°C/gas mark 3.

Place a large frying pan over a medium to high heat. Add the oil and brown the beef all over until it is uniformly dark and richly coloured. If you have 2 pieces of beef, fry them one at a time.

Place the beef in the roasting tin and roast for 15 minutes per 500g. When a temperature probe inserted into the centre reads 55°C the meat is done. Remove the beef from the roasting tin, set it on a plate and leave it to cool.

Once the beef is cold wrap it very tightly with cling film, winding it around snugly to compress the meat. This will make it easier to slice.

Leave the beef to chill for 2–3 days. To serve, slice it as thinly as you can and enjoy it with a watercress salad.

BEER-CURED BACON

✱ Cures 4–5kg ✱ Preparation time 5 minutes ✱ Cooking time 15 minutes plus overnight cooling time
✱ Curing time 4 days for the belly, 6 days for the loin

Pork belly and pork loin are cured for four and six days respectively. The resulting bacon
can be sliced and frozen in small portions or poached in a single piece and eaten cold with
pickles. This recipe uses a small amount of saltpetre. However, you can omit this if you
prefer. The colour will be less pink but there will be no loss of flavour.

4.5 litres beer

700g sea salt

450g soft brown sugar

2 tsp allspice berries

2 tsp black peppercorns

30cm piece free-range pork loin
and belly (ask your butcher to
separate the loin from the belly,
removing the bones. Once boned,
the combined weight will be
around 5kg)

10g saltpetre (optional) or salt

special equipment

2 large plastic tubs with tightly
fitting lids

Put the beer, salt, 400g brown sugar, allspice berries
and peppercorns into a large stainless steel pan over a high
heat. Bring to a boil and simmer for 2 minutes, ensuring that
all the salt and sugar have dissolved. Remove from the heat
and leave to cool. Once completely cooled, pour it into a large
plastic tub with a tightly fitting lid and chill overnight.

The next day mix together the saltpetre or salt with the
remaining brown sugar and rub it into the cut side of the
meat. Then place the meat with the cut sides facing each
other in another large tub. Cover and chill overnight.

The following day, pour the cold brine over the meat and
store, chilled, for 4 days. Turn the meat daily, ensuring that it
stays submerged in the brine.

After 4 days, remove the belly piece but leave the loin in the
brine. Pat the belly dry with kitchen paper and place on a wire
rack over a plastic tray in the fridge. Leave it there, uncovered,
overnight. Stand the loin on its edge, so that only the thickest
part is submerged. Leave for another 2 days to finish curing,
then drain, pat dry and leave, uncovered, in the fridge in the
same way as for the belly.

When the cured meat has dried overnight, slice thinly for
bacon or thickly for bacon steaks, which are excellent grilled
and served with lentils or yellow split peas.

PIG CHEEK JELLY

✷ Serves 8 ✷ Preparation time 10 minutes ✷ Curing time 4 days ✷ Rinsing time 1 day
✷ Cooking time 4 hours plus chilling overnight

Pig cheeks have a delicious, strong, meaty flavour. They are easily obtained and much easier to handle at home than a whole head, which is what Mrs Beeton would have used. The cheeks are brined, cooked and shredded with aromatics to form a jellied meat.

2 litres cider or water

200g sea salt

50g brown sugar

4 blades mace

10 black peppercorns

4–5 pigs' cheeks, boned, skin on

1 stick celery, trimmed and cut into chunks

1 large onion, peeled and cut into chunks

1 medium carrot, peeled and cut into chunks

2 bay leaves

4 allspice berries

1 clove

2 sheets gelatine

small bunch parsley, chopped

1 garlic clove, crushed

1 tsp red wine vinegar

salt and freshly ground black pepper

To make the brine set a large pan over a high heat and add the cider or water, salt, sugar, mace and peppercorns. Bring to a boil then remove from the heat. Once cool, pour the brine into a large bowl, add the pigs' cheeks, cover and chill. After 4 days, lift out the cheeks and discard the brine. Place the cheeks into a large bowl of water, cover and chill overnight.

The next day, remove the cheeks from the water and place in a large saucepan. Cover with fresh cold water and set over a high heat. Bring the pan to a simmer and taste the water. If it is very salty, discard it and boil the cheeks again with fresh water. When the water is boiling, add the celery, onion, carrot, bay leaves, allspice berries and the clove. Simmer over a very low heat for 1½ hours, or until the cheeks are tender and beginning to fall apart. Remove from the heat and leave the cheeks in the liquid. When they are cool enough to handle, shred the meat into a serving bowl, discarding the fat and skin. You should end up with approximately 370–400g meat.

Pour just over 500ml of the cooking liquid into a large measuring jug and skim off and discard any fat that floats to the surface with a large spoon. Then pour the cooking liquid into a saucepan and place it over a low heat.

Soak the gelatine sheets in cold water for 10 minutes, or until soft. Squeeze out any excess water and then add them to the warm cooking liquid, stirring to dissolve. Stir in the parsley, garlic and red wine vinegar. Season to taste, and then stir it thoroughly into the meat. Cover with cling film and chill. Once the jelly has set, serve it with good bread and piccalilli.

STOCKS &
LEFTOVERS

DARK CHICKEN STOCK

✳ Makes 1.5 litres ✳ Preparation time 1 hour 15 minutes ✳ Cooking time 6 hours

This full-flavoured chicken stock is made from browned, roasted chicken bones and pieces. It has an intense flavour and light gelatinous body and is excellent with strongly flavoured poultry and game dishes that can stand up to a robust stock.

1.5kg chicken wings and thighs

2 tbsp sunflower oil

1 large carrot, roughly chopped

2 onions, roughly chopped

2 sticks celery, roughly chopped

2 bay leaves

small bunch thyme

special equipment

a roasting tin and a large stockpot

Preheat the oven to 220°C/gas mark 7. Arrange the chicken wings and thighs in a roasting tin and set in the oven. Cook, turning occasionally, for 1 hour, or until the pieces are deep golden-brown in colour.

When the chicken is nearly cooked, place the oil in a large stockpot over medium heat. Add vegetables and fry until lightly coloured. Add the cooked chicken to the pan. Pour off and discard any excess fat in the roasting tin.

Pour a little water into the roasting tin and stir, scraping up any caramelised juices. Pour these into the pan with the vegetables and chicken.

Finally, add the herbs to the chicken and vegetables and pour enough cold water into the stockpot to cover the chicken and vegetables to a depth of 10cm. Turn the heat to high and bring the stock to a simmer, then reduce the heat. Make sure the stock does not boil at any point and skim off any scum that rises to the surface while it is simmering.

After 5 hours, strain the stock through a fine sieve or chinois into a large bowl. Leave it to cool, then cover and chill.

Once it is completely cold, carefully remove any fat from the top. Pour the stock back into the cleaned stockpot, place over a high heat and bring to a boil. Reduce the stock until you are left with 1.5 litres. Remove from the heat to cool, then chill until cold, pour into re-sealable 250ml containers and freeze for up to 2 months. To use, allow the stock to thaw out.

LIGHT CHICKEN STOCK

✳ Makes 1.5 litres ✳ Preparation time 10 minutes ✳ Cooking time 3 hours

Light chicken stock is used in delicately flavoured dishes, which would be masked by a more intensely flavoured stock. It is also useful for lighter soups, or for braising young vegetables such as turnips or beetroot.

1.5kg chicken wings and thighs, raw

1 large carrot, roughly chopped

2 onions, roughly chopped

2 sticks celery, roughly chopped

2 bay leaves

small bunch thyme

special equipment

a large stockpot

Place all the ingredients into the stockpot over a medium heat. Cover with cold water to a depth of 5–10cm and bring to a gentle simmer. Continue to simmer for 2 hours, making sure the stock does not boil at any point and skimming as necessary. Strain the stock through a fine sieve or chinois into a large bowl. Leave it to cool, then cover and chill.

Carefully remove any fat from the top of the chilled stock and pour it back into the cleaned stockpot. Bring to a boil over a high heat to reduce the stock until you are left with 1.5 litres. Remove from the heat and cool, then pour into re-sealable 250ml containers and freeze for up to 2 months.

JELLIED BEEF STOCK

✳ Makes 2 litres ✳ Preparation time 1 hour 15 minutes
✳ Cooking time 12 hours 30 mintues first day, 4 hours second day

This stock is best started early in the morning so that it has plenty of time to cook. It can then be cooled overnight and reduced the following day to give a rich, unctuous stock.

5kg beef or veal bones

4 tbsp oil

1 large carrot, roughly chopped

1 stick celery, roughly chopped

1 large onion, roughly chopped

3 garlic cloves, peeled

1 bay leaf

100g large mushrooms or mushroom trimmings, roughly chopped

1 tomato, roughly chopped

300ml light red wine

1 pig's trotter, split in half

small bunch thyme

1 small tarragon sprig

1 tsp black peppercorns

special equipment

2 roasting tins and a large stockpot

Preheat the oven to 220°C/gas mark 7.

Arrange the bones in the roasting tins and roast for 1 hour, turning occasionally so that they brown evenly, then remove from the oven and pour off any melted fat for roasties (see page 88). Then place the oil in the stockpot and set it over a medium heat. Add the carrot, celery and onion and cook, stirring, for about 10–15 minutes, or until well caramelised.

Add the garlic, bay leaf, mushrooms and tomato and continue to cook until the mixture is almost dry and beginning to stick to the pan. Add the red wine and continue cooking until it has reduced by half, scraping all the sediment from the bottom of the pan. Add the trotter to the pan along with 2 litres of cold water, then add half the roasted bones. Give everything a good stir before adding the remaining bones and another 4 litres of cold water, or enough to cover the bones well.

Turn the heat to high and bring the stock to a simmer, but do not allow it to boil. Skim to remove any scum that rises to the surface, and add the herbs and peppercorns. Continue to simmer without boiling for 12 hours, skimming as necessary. Strain the stock through a very fine sieve or chinois into a large bowl and allow it to cool overnight.

The next morning, remove and discard any fat, and pour the stock back into the cleaned stockpot. Boil and reduce, skimming as necessary, until you are left with 2 litres. Remove the stockpot from the heat and leave to cool. Chill until cold then pour into re-sealable 250ml containers and freeze for up to 2 months. To use, allow the stock to thaw out then dilute with an equal quantity of water for a full-flavoured beef stock.

LEFTOVER MUTTON BROTH

✳ Serves 4 ✳ Preparation time 10 minutes ✳ Cooking time 30 minutes

Inspired by both Mrs Beeton's mutton soup and her preoccupation with economy in the kitchen, this recipe has been added to make the most of the leftovers from the braised mutton recipe on page 51. It is only truly practical to make this broth if it is in combination with that dish.

leftover meat, stock, barley and vegetables

1 tbsp sunflower oil

1 onion, peeled and finely chopped

1 carrot, peeled and finely chopped

1 leek, halved and finely sliced

1 stick celery, trimmed and finely chopped

1 bay leaf

1 potato, peeled and cut into 1cm dice

small bunch fresh parsley, leaves only, chopped, to garnish

salt and freshly ground black pepper

Start by assessing what you have left from the braised mutton dish. You need to make sure that you have enough stock and flavoursome barley to make this soup. Do this by taking the leftover barley from the mutton braise and pouring it into a sieve over a large bowl and collecting any stock that drains through. Pick over the leftover mutton and strip out and discard any fat. Chop the meat into small pieces. Measure the stock, meat and barley. The exact quantity of meat is not essential – the more the better, but you will probably end up with about 250g combined meat and barley. You will need approximately 500ml stock, so if you are short, add a little light chicken stock (see page 69) or vegetable stock to make up the quantity. If there are any vegetables left over from the braise, dice them and set them aside.

You are now ready to make the soup. Place the oil in a saucepan over medium heat. Add the onion, carrot, leek, celery, a pinch of salt, a grinding of black pepper and the bay leaf and cook until the vegetables soften but do not colour at the edges. If they do start to catch, add a splash of water and turn the heat down. This will take about 10 minutes.

When the vegetables are soft, add the 500ml stock and 400ml water and bring to a simmer. Cook for about 5 minutes then add the potato. Simmer for 5–10 minutes, or until the potato is almost cooked, then add the chopped meat, barley and leftover vegetables. Warm the soup through, adjust the seasoning with salt and black pepper and add a little water if necessary. Garnish with the parsley and serve.

CLARIFYING STOCKS

✳ To clarify 2 litres of stock ✳ Preparation time 10 minutes ✳ Cooking time 20–30 minutes

Clarification is a method used to clear stocks that have clouded or need to be refined for use in a consommé. Mrs Beeton noted that, 'when [a stock] is obliged to be clarified it is deteriorated both in quality and flavour', yet she did include a recipe for clarifying stocks, which calls for a simple mixture of egg whites and water, in her book. This updated recipe uses a similar method, but retains the flavour by using a mixture of minced, lean meat of the same type as the stock being clarified, plus vegetables, herbs and spices. You need to start with cold stock so that the egg white solidifies gradually, trapping particles from the stock as it does so.

2 litres cold chicken or beef stock (see pages 68–69 or 70)

120g egg white (about 3 large or 4 medium egg whites)

30g carrot, peeled and roughly chopped

50g onion, peeled and roughly chopped

20g celery, trimmed and roughly chopped

20g leek, trimmed and roughly chopped

200g lean, minced chicken or beef

few thyme sprigs

1 bay leaf

1 garlic clove, peeled

1 tsp black peppercorns

Place the cold stock into a large saucepan. Put the egg white, vegetables and meat in the jug of a food processor and pulse to chop to a coarse paste.

Turn the heat under the saucepan to high and whisk the vegetable and egg paste, the herbs, garlic and peppercorns into the stock. Bring to a gentle simmer over a high heat, whisking again once or twice as it warms. At no point should the stock be allowed to bubble.

As the stock reaches a simmer, the egg and vegetables begin to form a thick scum on the surface. Reduce the heat to low and keep the stock just under a simmer. The surface layer will thicken and set, trapping all of the sediment and debris.

After 10 minutes, remove the pan from heat and break a hole in the egg crust large enough to fit the bowl of a ladle through. Very carefully ladle the stock out through the hole and into a muslin-lined sieve suspended over a large bowl.

Cover and chill immediately and use as required. This will yield approximately 1.8 litres, and freezes for up to 2 months.

ON THE
TABLE

A Note on Sauces

The purpose of a sauce is to complement food. Always be careful to match the right sauce to the right food so that the sauce never dominates. When seasoning a sauce aim for an assertive, but not salty, finish.

Mrs Beeton offers plenty of suggestions for sides and sauces to enjoy with classic meat dishes, so whether you fancy brilliant pickled shallots to serve with cold pork pies or cheese (see page 84), or the best ever tomato chutney (page 81), to enjoy with Sunday brunch, this chapter is full of inspiring treats.

Making gravy

Gravy is the sauce made from the caramelised juices of roasted meat left behind in the roasting tin. Adding wine and/or stock to this makes the gravy base, but if you are using wine, allow it to boil for a minute to burn off the alcohol first. Then thicken the liquid with beurre manié, or cornflour or arrowroot mixed with a little water. Simmer, stirring, to loosen any caramelised bits still adhering to the roasting tin, and to allow the thickener to finish cooking. When the gravy has cooked, allow it to sit for a minute then spoon off any fat that floats to the surface, or use a separating jug.

Setting jams and jellies

Before beginning your jelly, put one or two saucers in the fridge to cool.

Mixtures of fruit or fruit juice and sugar will come to a boil at a temperature over 100°C. As the water is driven off by boiling, the temperature will increase and the sugar concentration will rise. To test for temperature, make sure that your thermometer or probe is held in the main body of the jelly. If it is held too near the bottom or top the reading will be inaccurate. As the mixture of fruit and sugar approaches 105°C, it will noticeably thicken, because at this point the pectin will begin to gel together to form a mesh. How long this takes depends on many factors, such as sugar content and acidity.

To test for a set, spoon a small amount of mixture onto one of the cold saucers you have placed in the fridge. Let it sit for a minute, then push the edge with your finger. You should notice that the surface wrinkles. If it does not, continue to cook the jam for a couple of minutes and then test it on a cold sauces again.

APPLE JELLY

✻ Makes approx 2.4kg – 5 or 6 jars ✻ Preparation time 20 minutes
✻ Cooking time 1 hour 30 minutes spread over 2 days

Bramleys have good acidity and make an excellent jelly – and this is a very handy one to
have in the larder. If you use a different variety of cooking apple, adjust the sugar to taste.

**2½kg Bramley apples,
freshly picked or slightly
under-ripe**

approx 1.6kg jam sugar

juice of 3 lemons

special equipment

**a sugar thermometer or
temperature probe**

Peel the apples and chop them into small pieces. Place in a
stainless steel pan and add enough cold water to just cover –
you will need about 2 litres. Bring to the boil over a high heat,
then simmer gently, topping up as necessary to ensure the
apples remain just covered, until the fruit is completely broken
down and soft. Strain the hot cooked apples through a jelly
bag or a muslin-lined sieve over a large bowl, and leave to drip
overnight if possible.

When you are ready to finish the jelly, place your clean jars on
a baking sheet in a cool oven at 120°C/gas mark ½, and place
a couple of saucers in the fridge for testing the set of the
jelly when finished. Measure the juice. For every 500ml juice,
weigh out 400g jam sugar. Place the juice and sugar in a large
pan over a high heat, stirring continuously until the sugar has
dissolved. Add the lemon juice, mix well and then divide the
mixture into two roughly equal parts (this will enable to you
to finish the jelly quickly, preserving the flavour).

Bring one half to a rapid rolling boil and cook until it reaches
105°C, stirring frequently to prevent sticking. Begin to test for
setting point when it starts to thicken, using the cold-saucer
test, opposite. Once a setting point has been reached, remove
the jelly from the heat and allow it to form a skin.

Remove and discard any scum that has formed and pot the
jelly into the sterilised jars. Cover with a waxed-paper disc
and seal with cellophane. Repeat with the remaining mixture.

HORSERADISH SAUCE

✳ Serves 8 ✳ Preparation time 10 minutes

Mrs Beeton recommends horseradish sauce a lot – and it almost sums up the British taste for piquant in one recipe. It is the perfect complement to a cold piece of beef or smoked fish – adding a little lemon zest gives a welcome freshness.

200ml double cream

½ tsp caster sugar

1 tsp white wine vinegar

½ tsp English mustard powder

50g piece fresh
horseradish root

lemon juice, to taste

½ tsp finely grated
lemon zest (optional)

salt and freshly ground
black pepper

Place the cream, a pinch of salt and the sugar, white wine vinegar and mustard powder in a large bowl and beat until the mixture begins to form soft peaks.

Peel the horseradish root and rub with a little lemon juice to prevent it going brown. Finely grate the root into the cream, stirring it in and tasting as you go. Stop when it is strong enough for your taste. Stir in the lemon zest, if using, and season to taste. Chill until ready to serve but use on the day of making.

APPLE SAUCE

✳ Serves 4 ✳ Preparation time 10 minutes ✳ Cooking time 15 minutes

Mrs Beeton would have used an old variety of apple for her sauce, but Bramleys work well here. The butter adds natural sweetness, while the new additions of bay and shallot lend a savoury note that appeal to the modern palate. Serve with cooked game, pork or poultry.

20g unsalted butter

1 shallot, peeled and
finely chopped

1 bay leaf

2 large cooking apples,
peeled, cored and chopped
into small pieces

pinch salt

sugar, to taste

Place the butter in a small saucepan over a medium heat. Add the shallot and bay leaf. Cook for 2–3 minutes, stirring. Add the finely chopped apple and cook until the apple begins to break down. Add a splash of water as the apple cooks to keep it just moist enough to prevent it catching or burning. Add the salt and a little sugar to taste. Continue to cook, stirring occasionally, until the apple is soft. Cool, remove the bay leaf and serve at room temperature.

APPLE CHUTNEY

✳ Makes approx 3.7kg – 8 to 10 jars ✳ Preparation time 25 minutes ✳ Cooking time 1 hour

Chutneys, along with many other spiced ketchups and sauces, were often brought home to the British kitchen by military gentlemen who had developed a taste for the exotic while overseas. We are now able to buy fresh spices imported monthly into Europe. This must be taken into consideration when looking at the quantities used in historic kitchens, where spices would have invariably taken many months to arrive from abroad, resulting in considerable loss of flavour. This chutney offers a superb way to use up a glut of apples. Its warm, autumnal spice mix, based largely on coriander seeds, works exceptionally well with apple.

2kg Bramley or other cooking apples, peeled and cored weight

1kg shallots, peeled and finely sliced

500g sultanas

300g soft brown sugar

300g granulated sugar

1 litre cider vinegar

2 tbsp whole coriander seeds

1 tsp ground ginger

1 tsp ground cinnamon

special equipment

a stainless steel preserving pan

Place the washed jars on a baking sheet in a cool oven, 120°C/gas mark ½.

Chop the apples into 1cm dice and add to a large stainless steel pan with all the other ingredients. Place the pan on a high heat and bring to a boil, stirring to dissolve the sugar. Simmer on a medium-high heat, stirring regularly, until the chutney is thick. This will take approximately 1 hour depending on the size of the pan and the surface area from which the liquid is evaporating. Take great care not to let the chutney burn – you will have to stir constantly as it begins to thicken, scraping the bottom of the pan carefully with a heatproof spatula or wooden spoon.

When the chutney is ready, place it into the sterilised jars. Seal and store in a cool, dark place for at least 1 month and then use within a year of making.

TOMATO CHUTNEY

✴ Makes approx 3kg – 7 jars ✴ Preparation time 25 minutes ✴ Cooking time 1 hour

Mrs Beeton provided many recipes for using up quantities of the many fruits that we are often faced with gluts of at the end of summer. She gave a recipe for a chutney that blended apple and tomato together, but as each of these fruits benefits from different spice treatments they are better preserved separately. This tomato chutney, with its bird's-eye chilli kick, is one of the best ever for eating with sausages for a weekend breakfast, or for enjoying in the autumn at a bonfire party.

2kg tomatoes, chopped into small pieces

1kg onions, peeled and chopped into small pieces

500g raisins

70g fresh root ginger, peeled and finely grated

6 garlic cloves, peeled and finely chopped

300g granulated sugar

300g soft brown sugar

1 tsp allspice berries

1 stick cinnamon

1 bird's-eye chilli, or other hot chilli, cut in half lengthwise

1 litre cider vinegar

special equipment

a large stainless steel preserving pan

Place several clean jars on a baking sheet in an oven preheated to 120°C/gas mark ½.

Place all the ingredients into a large stainless steel pan and bring to the boil, stirring to dissolve sugar. Turn down the heat and simmer, stirring constantly, until the chutney has thickened. This will take approximately 1 hour depending on the size of your pan and the surface area from which the liquid is evaporating. Take great care not to let the chutney burn. As it begins to thicken, scrape the bottom of the pan carefully with a heatproof spatula or wooden spoon to prevent it catching.

When the chutney is ready, pot it into the sterilised jars. Seal and store in a cool, dark place for at least 1 month and then use within 1 year.

RASPBERRY VINEGAR

✳ Makes approx 2 litres ✳ Preparation time 10 minutes over 3 days

Mrs Beeton used raspberry vinegar diluted with water as a tonic. In fact, because it is so intensely fruity, it also makes a super addition to dressings or to game dishes. Try using a splash when cooking liver – it is a delicious combination.

1.5kg raspberries

1kg caster sugar

1 litre white wine vinegar or cider vinegar

special equipment

a large stainless steel or ceramic bowl and a jelly bag or muslin

Place the raspberries in a large stainless steel or ceramic bowl and crush lightly. Add the sugar and the vinegar and cover. Steep together for 3 days and then strain the vinegar through a colander lined with muslin suspended over a large bowl. Alternatively, use a jelly bag and stand. Transfer the vinegar into vinegar bottles that have non-reactive seals. Store in a cool, dark place for at least 1 month, and then use within 1 year.

PARSLEY & GARLIC BUTTER

✳ Makes 100g ✳ Preparation time 5 minutes

Mrs Beeton's parsley butter was suggested as an accompaniment to boiled fowls – which we rarely cook today. However, the addition of a little garlic turns the original recipe into a versatile butter for the modern kitchen. It is whipped to ensure that it does not run when heated.

100g softened unsalted butter

large bunch of parsley, leaves only, finely chopped

2 garlic cloves, finely chopped

½ tsp Maldon or other flaky salt

Place the butter in a medium-sized bowl and whip until creamy, pale and fluffy. Add the parsley, garlic and salt and whip until combined.

Cover and chill until required. It will keep for 2 days in the fridge.

PICKLED SHALLOTS

✳ Makes approx 2kg ✳ Preparation time 1 hour plus overnight brining ✳ Cooking time 20 minutes

These classic pickled shallots are excellent with Mrs Beeton's pork pie – make them when shallots are at their peak in the late summer because they don't store well – or use baby onions. If you like a spicier pickle, add a couple of chillies to the spiced vinegar. Mrs Beeton cooked her pickled onions to remove their strength, but today we prefer them pickled raw and full of bite.

20g salt

2kg shallots

for the spiced pickling vinegar

800ml cider vinegar

200ml white wine vinegar

200ml water

5g blade mace

5g coriander seeds

5g allspice berries

2 bay leaves

2 cinnamon sticks

10g mustard seeds

200g granulated sugar

special equipment

a large stainless steel preserving pan

Add the salt to 2 litres of water in a large pan, place over a medium heat and stir to dissolve. Remove from the heat and leave to cool.

Soak the shallots in their skins in a large bowl of warm water, and begin to peel them, trimming the tips and removing the roots carefully, so that you leave the root plates intact. This will help to stop the shallots falling apart.

Place the peeled shallots in the cooled brine, cover and leave to soak overnight.

Put all of the ingredients for the spiced vinegar in a large stainless steel pan. Bring to a simmer over a high heat, stirring to dissolve the sugar, then leave to cool overnight.

The next day, remove the shallots from the brine and rinse. Pack the shallots into clean and dry preserving jars (there is no need to sterilise if you are using non-reactive lids). Pour in the spiced vinegar, ensuring that the liquid covers all the shallots and that there are no air bubbles. Seal and store in a cool, dark place for at least 1 month and then use within 1 year of making.

PICKLED BEETROOT

✱ Makes approx 1.6kg – 4 or 5 jars ✱ Preparation time 15 minutes ✱ Cooking time 1–2 hours

Make this pickle in the late summer when the beetroot are mature and taste their best. Rather than boil the beetroot, I roast them to concentrate their flavour, and I use a mildly spiced vinegar to cure them, which gives the pickled beetroot an aromatic edge.

1kg unpeeled young beetroots

20 juniper berries

salt, to taste

for the spiced pickling vinegar

300ml cider vinegar

200ml white wine vinegar

70ml water

½ tsp coriander seeds

1 tsp allspice berries

2 tsp juniper berries

½ tsp blade mace

2 bay leaves

200g granulated sugar

special equipment

a roasting tin

Preheat the oven to 200°C/gas mark 6.

Top and tail beetroot, wash them well, and place them in a roasting tin lined with foil. Add the juniper berries and a generous pinch or two of salt, cover with another sheet of foil and seal very tightly on all sides. Put the roasting tin in the oven and cook for 1–2 hours, depending on size, until the beetroot are cooked through and tender.

While the beetroot are cooking, place all the ingredients for the pickling vinegar into a pan, bring to a boil and simmer for 5 minutes. Leave to cool.

Once the beetroot are cooked, remove them from the oven and leave to cool. Reduce the oven temperature to 120°C/gas mark ½ and place 4–5 jars into the oven to sterilise for half an hour. When the beetroot are cool, peel them, cut each into 8 even pieces and put into the jars. Cover with spiced pickling vinegar, seal the jars and store in a cool, dark place for at least 1 month and use within 1 year.

ROAST POTATOES

✳ Serves 4 ✳ Preparation time 30 minutes ✳ Cooking time 1 hour 30 minutes

Mrs Beeton only mentioned roast potatoes in passing: she cooked them in front of the fire, and noted that they should be sent to the table with additional cold butter. Of course, it is now more convenient to roast potatoes inside the oven according to the instructions in this recipe.

800g peeled potatoes cut into 3–4cm cubes

100g goose fat or dripping

salt

special equipment

a large roasting tin

Preheat the oven to 220°C/gas mark 7.

Place the potatoes in a large saucepan over a medium to high heat and cover them with water. Add 1 tsp salt and bring to a light boil. After 15 minutes remove from the heat and drain well. Shake the colander a few times to ruffle the edges of the potatoes, which will give them a crisper skin after roasting.

When you are ready to roast the potatoes, put the goose fat or dripping in the roasting tin and place in the oven just until the fat melts, then arrange the potatoes in the melted fat and return the tin to the oven. Turn the potatoes every 20 minutes. After 60 minutes, reduce the heat to 180°C/gas mark 4 and cook for a further 30 minutes, or until the potatoes are crisp and brown.

Meanwhile, line a baking tray with kitchen paper and keep it handy near the oven. When the potatoes have finished roasting, remove them from the oven and switch the oven off. Using a pair of tongs, lift the potatoes out of the fat and onto the prepared baking tray. Place them back in the oven for 5 minutes to finish draining and serve.

YORKSHIRE PUDDINGS

✳ Makes 24 small Yorkshire puddings
✳ Preparation time 10 minutes plus 10 minutes resting time ✳ Cooking time 20–25 minutes

Mrs Beeton made her Yorkshire pudding in a large shallow tin and then cut it into squares before serving. Her choice of cooking fat was beef dripping, and she also liked to stand the Yorkshire pudding tin under the meat as it cooked to collect the juices. To speed up the cooking time and for ease of portioning, this recipe is for small individual puddings, made in muffin trays, and they are best served piping hot with lots of gravy.

225g plain flour

600ml milk

3 medium eggs

large pinch salt

25g butter, melted

50g lard or dripping, to cook

special equipment

2 x 12-hole muffin trays

Preheat the oven to 220°C/gas mark 7. Mix the flour, milk and eggs together with the salt in a bowl. Whisk until the batter is free of lumps. Leave to stand in a cool place for 10 minutes or until required. Strain the batter through a fine sieve into a jug and stir in the melted butter along with 3 tbsp cold water.

Set out two 12-hole muffin trays and place a small knob of lard or dripping into each hole, then place in the oven until the fat has melted and is hot but not smoking.

Remove the trays from the oven and carefully divide the batter between the holes. Bake the puddings for 10–15 minutes, or until they are well-risen and golden brown. Serve immediately.

PRODUCERS & SUPPLIERS

Spices

Green Saffron Spices

Unit 16, Knockgriffin, Midleton, Cork, Ireland

Tel 00 353 21 463 7960

www.greensaffron.com

Arun and Olive Kapil's family business imports and grinds premium spices from family farms across India.

Meat

Anna's Happy Trotters

Burland, Holme Farm, Howden,
East Yorkshire DN14 7LY

Tel 01430 433 030

www.annashappytrotters.com

Delicious and well butchered Yorkshire free-range pork from one of our finest pig farmers, Anna Longthorp.

The Blackface Meat Company

Weatherall Foods Limited, Crochmore House, Irongray, Dumfries DG2 9SF

Tel 01387 730 326

www.blackface.co.uk

This small family business rears Blackface sheep and Galloway cattle in the south west of Scotland. Their superb mutton, lamb, game, beef and pork is produced with care and attention.

Borrowdale Herdwick

Yew Tree Farm, Rosthwaite, Borrowdale,
Cumbria CA12 5XB

Tel: 01768 777 675

www.borrowdaleherdwick.co.uk

A small farm rearing the area's traditional Herdwick sheep, where the animals enjoy a full life, slowly growing on the beautiful fells of Borrowdale. The animals are available as hogget or mutton. Their rich, nutty flavour is exceptional.

The Dexter Cattle Society

www.dextercattle.co.uk

The Dexter Cattle Society helps farmers find markets and buyers for their cattle and keeps a directory of suppliers and locations where this fantastic beef can be purchased.

Graig Farm

Dolau, Llandrindod Wells,
Powys LD1 5TL

Tel 01686 627 979

www.graigfarm.co.uk

This farm supplies a wide range of organic products, including meat and poultry, from its online shop. All of their produce is cared for to high standards.

Langley Chase Organic Farm

Kington Langley,
Wiltshire SN15 5PW

Tel 01249 750 095

www.langleychase.co.uk

A small organic farm producing award-winning Manx Loaghtan lamb and mutton which is truly delicious and unique.

Pipers Farm

Cullompton,

Devon EX15 1SD

Tel 01392 881 380

www.pipersfarm.com

Pipers Farm helps to sustain 30 farming families who have nurtured the Devon countryside for generations. With a commitment to growing the best and healthiest meat, Peter and Henri Greig set up the farm over 20 years ago, and use traditional methods of farming to offer the higest standards of animal welfare. Their range of products, including red ruby beef, venison, pies and casseroles, can be ordered online for next day delivery.

Rhug Estate

Corwen, Denbighshire LL21 0EH

Tel 01490 413 000

www.rhug.co.uk

An organic farm and butchery supplying a variety of meat including Aberdeen Angus beef, Salt Marsh lamb, chicken, game and traditional Duroc pork. All the meat (with the exception of the game, which is sourced as locally as possible) is organic and comes from their own farms.

SausageMaking.org

0845 643 6915

www.sausagemaking.org

An online site that sells all you need to make your own bacon, sausages, salami and hams.

Equipment

Lakeland

Alexandra Buildings,
Windermere,
Cumbria LA23 1BQ

Tel 0153 948 8100

www.lakeland.co.uk

Lakeland provides an array of innovative cookware, appliances and utensils. The company places enormous value on customer satisfaction, and uses customer feedback to develop its vast range.

Nisbets Catering Equipment

Fourth Way,
Avonmouth,
Bristol BS11 8TB

Tel 0845 140 5555

www.nisbets.co.uk

This is one of the UK's largest suppliers of catering equipment, and a great source of larger scale cooking equipment such as stock pots.

Useful organisations

FARMA

Lower Ground Floor, 12 Southgate Street, Winchester, Hampshire SO23 9EF

Tel 0845 45 88 420

www.farmersmarkets.net

The National Farmers' Retail & Markets Association represents the sale of local food and fresh farm products direct to the public through farmers' markets and farm shops. Visit their website for a list of certified markets and suppliers in your area.

Freedom Food Limited

Wilberforce Way,
Southwater, Horsham,
West Sussex RH139RS

Tel 0300 123 0014

www.rspca.org.uk/freedomfood

Freedom Food is the RSPCA's farm assurance and food labelling scheme. It is the only UK farm assurance scheme to focus solely on improving the welfare of farm animals reared for food.

Slow Food UK

Slow Food UK, 6 Neal's Yard, Covent Garden, London WC2H 9DP

Tel 020 7099 1132

www.slowfood.org.uk

Slow Food UK is part of the global Slow Food movement. It has thousands of members and connections with local groups around the UK that link the pleasure of artisan food to community and the environment.

Soil Association

South Plaza, Marlborough Street,
Bristol BS1 3NX

Tel 0117 314 5000

www.soilassociation.org

The Soil Association is a charity campaigning for planet-friendly food and farming. It offers guidance to consumers looking for local suppliers of organic food as well as advice for organic growers and businesses.

GLOSSARY OF COOKING TERMS

Many languages have influenced the British kitchen, but none so much as French – hardly surprising since French food has often been held up as the benchmark for excellence, in Mrs Beeton's time as well as in our own. Long before the Michelin guide began to report on British restaurants, French chefs were working for British royalty and could be found in the kitchens of many large country houses. Perhaps the most famous of these was Antonin Carême, chef to the Prince Regent (later George IV), who set the standard for future chefs to emulate. Mrs Beeton knew of him by name and reputation. The list below is intended to help explain the more commonly used terms – many, but not all, of which come from the French.

baste   to moisten meat or poultry during the roasting process by pouring over fat or liquid

beurre manie   a paste made from butter and flour that is used to thicken hot sauces

bone   to remove the bones from fish, meat or poultry

brine   a saltwater solution used for preserving and pickling

brown   to colour the surface of a food by cooking it in hot fat, caramelising the sugars and developing flavour

butter muslin   a fine cotton cloth used for straining jellies, stocks and dairy products. It should be scalded before use.

casserole   a deep, lidded cooking pot made from an ovenproof material

chine   to separate the backbone from the ribs in a joint of meat, to make carving easier

chinois   a conical sieve with a very fine mesh used for straining soups, sauces and purées to give a very smooth result

clarify   (of stock) to remove sediment or filter using egg white (see page 73)

clarified butter   pure butterfat, made by heating butter and lifting the fat from the liquid milk that forms underneath. Clarified butter does not burn as easily as butter and has a longer shelf life

cure   to preserve fish or meat by salting, smoking or drying

deep fat fry   to cook food by immersing it in oil

de-glaze   to add liquid to a pan after roasting or sautéeing in order to dissolve any juices or sediment left in the base of the pan, picking up their flavour

devil   to cook with spicy seasoning

dripping   the fat which drips from meat, poultry or game during cooking

flambé or flame   to remove the alcohol from hot food by lighting the fumes

gravy   a sauce made from the juices exuded from meat, poultry or game during cooking, combined with stock or water and starch

green bacon   unsmoked bacon, may be either from the loin or belly

griskin   backbone, spine or chine of pork

hang   to suspend meat or game in a cool, dry place until matured and tenderised

hogget   a sheep aged between one and two years of age

joint   to cut an animal or piece of meat into smaller pieces by cutting through the joints to separate the bones. Also a piece of meat for roasting

lard   natural or refined pork fat

larding   threading strips of fat through lean meat before cooking, to add flavour and prevent the flesh from drying out

marbled   (of meat) containing intramuscular, as opposed to surface, fat

marinade   a mixture of oil, wine or vinegar used to tenderise or flavour meat

medallions   round pieces of meat, usually of steak or loin, usually fried

mirepoix   a mixture of finely chopped vegetables, usually onion, carrot and celery

mutton   the name given to sheep that are over two years old at slaughter

pâté   a cooked meat or vegetable puree

pickle   to preserve meat or vegetables in brine or vinegar

purée   food that has been blended or passed through a sieve to give a smooth texture

ramekin   a small ceramic, ovenproof dish, often used for soufflés or creams

reduce   to concentrate a liquid, for example a sauce or stock, by boiling it until a portion has evaporated

render   to slowly cook meat and trimmings so that they release their fat

sauté   to fry food in hot shallow fat, turning it frequently, until it is evenly browned

score   to cut shallow gashes into the surface of food before cooking

sear   to brown meat rapidly using a fierce heat to seal in the juices

seasoned flour   flour mixed with salt and pepper, and sometimes other spices, often used to coat meat or fish before cooking

season   to add salt, pepper, spices, herbs or other ingredients to food to add flavour or (at the end of the cooking time) to correct the balance of flavours

sediment   a solid residue left in the bottom of a tin after roasting meat or poultry

skewer   a metal or wooden stick used to hold food in place during cooking

skillet   a heavy cast iron frying pan

soused   pickled in brine or vinegar

steep   to soak in liquid, in order to hydrate

suet   a hard fat from around the kidneys of animals, usually cattle

sweetbreads   a collective name for the pancreas and thyroid glands of animals, usually lambs or calves

truss   to tie a bird or piece of meat into a neat shape using string

whip   to beat eggs or cream until they are thick and increased in volume

INDEX

ACKNOWLEDGEMENTS

Mum, Sandra Baker, helped without question in the kitchen and office both in the process of testing the recipes and in organising manuscripts – you are a blessing.

To my sister Louise, and to Oscar and Fanny for providing moral support go hearty thanks. Much respect and love goes to Dad, John Baker, for being such a lover of shooting and game who has provided us with a wonderful supply of delicious food for so many years.

Adam Sellar provided great support in the kitchen during the testing of the recipes – thank you.

Amanda Harris and Debbie Woska sat through the creation of *Mrs Beeton How to Cook* with me – providing just the right amount of support and encouragement – thank you. Zelda Turner deserves thanks for helping trim and sculpt the recipes in this smaller collection.

To all the design team – Julyan Bayes, Lucie Steriker, Sammy-Jo Squire and her crew, and the photographer Andrew Hayes-Watkins and his team for making the book look so beautiful. The team behind the scenes at Orion helped enormously – Elizabeth Allen and Nicky Carswell especially.

Suppliers and helpers were many – but chiefly thanks go to Mike Wilson and his team in Patrington for supplying me with superb beef and lamb in quantity for so many years, and to Anna Longthorp for producing the best pork you can buy.

Gerard Baker